Why
CATHOLICS
DON'T GIVE
...And What Can Be Done About It

UPDATED

Why
CATHOLICS DON'T GIVE
...And What Can Be Done About It

CHARLES E. ZECH

Introduction by
FRANCIS J. BUTLER

Our Sunday Visitor Publishing Division
Our Sunday Visitor, Inc.
Huntington, Indiana 46750

Copyright © 2000, 2006 by Our Sunday Visitor Publishing Division, Our Sunday Visitor, Inc. Published 2006

11 10 09 08 07 06   1 2 3 4 5 6 7 8 9

Our Sunday Visitor Publishing Division
Our Sunday Visitor, Inc.
200 Noll Plaza
Huntington, IN 46750

ISBN-13: 978-1-59276-261-3
ISBN-10: 1-59276-261-1 (Inventory No. T314)
LCCN: 2006923565

Cover design by Rebecca J. Heaston
Interior design by Sherri L. Hoffman

PRINTED IN THE UNITED STATES OF AMERICA

CONTENTS

ACKNOWLEDGEMENTS

This study could not have been possible without a great deal of support, assistance, and advice. Major funding came from the Lilly Endowment, Inc., a private foundation interested in the study of religion. They generously supported this work with two separate grants. The first underwrote my participation in The American Congregational Giving Study, and the second allowed me to focus just on the data for Catholics in our sample and write this book. While the entire Lilly staff has been a delight to work with, I'm especially grateful for the encouragement and support offered by Fred Hofheinz, Program Officer in Religion at Lilly.

Many of my views on religious giving were sharpened while I was a participant in the Project on Non-Profit Organizations at Yale University, another Lilly-funded project. All of the members of that seminar contributed to the development of my understanding of religious giving, but I am especially grateful for the insights gained from discussions with Scott Cormode, Jim Davidson, Thom Jeavons, Greg Krohn, and David Roozen.

Pete Zaleski, my colleague and frequent coauthor from Villanova's Economics Department, has been patient and generous with his time in answering my questions about various statistical methodologies. Dave Reid, a stewardship and development professional, read a draft of the manuscript and offered valuable advice from his unique perspective.

My undergraduate research assistant, John Cacchione, and my graduate assistants, Ricardo Martinez and Dennis McCafferty, were all wonderfully understanding in meeting short deadlines and consistently provided me with superior quality work.

This study relied on the data collected from the Lilly-funded American Congregational Giving Study. I am grateful to the bishops in the nine

U.S. dioceses where data collection took place for their cooperation; to the 125 parish pastors who completed the parish profile surveys and enabled us to survey their parishioners; and to the nearly 2,200 Catholic laypersons who returned completed surveys. This was an enormous project, and was truly a team effort among Dean Hoge, Patrick McNamara, Michael Donahue, and myself. Together we developed and tested the survey materials. We spent many hours convening in person and in conference calls, bouncing ideas off one another. Each of us was responsible for the actual data collection in various parts of the country. Our many discussions were instrumental in helping to frame my interpretation of the data. For all of these reasons, even though I am responsible for the writing of this book and the interpretations that appear in it, the book is written using the comradely "we" in recognition of their contribution. But, for heaven's sake, don't blame them for any errors or misinterpretations that appear.

My wife, Ann, herself an economist and graduate theology student, served as a sounding board and filter for my analysis, and offered me the type of encouragement that no one else could. My children, Tom, Trish, John, and Ron, graciously gave up time with their dad and (sometimes begrudgingly) occasionally took over my share of the household chores while I worked on this book.

To the extent that this book is part of my own faith journey, I acknowledge a special debt of gratitude to my small faith community: Ann, Bob, Rosemary, Glenn, Marian, Tim, Kathleen, Anna, Lois, Bill, Ellie, and Margaret. They have been a constant source of inspiration, always moving me in the right direction, both through their example and their wisdom. They represent the best of everything that the Catholic Church has to offer. It is to them that this book is dedicated.

— CHARLES ZECH
VILLANOVA, PENNSYLVANIA
MARCH 1999

INTRODUCTION TO THE SECOND EDITION

This is a time of sharp contrasts in Catholic life. Never before have so many in our parish pews been considered financially comfortable. Yet, with news stories of diocesan bankruptcies and a ceaseless spate of parish and school closings in many parts of the country, one would never suspect that Catholics are prospering.

The baby-boomer, post-World War II generation is entering its retirement years right now, and it does so from positions of unprecedented material advantage. It is estimated that wealth passing through the hands of this generation to their progeny will total some $41 trillion.

New affluence and the social mobility that accompanies it have meant that Catholics are participating at the elite levels of American society. They represent the largest segment of the U.S. Congress by faith affiliation. Catholics can be counted in numbers disproportionate to their percentage in the general U.S. population among the leaders of America's Fortune 500 companies, and armies of their children fill the classrooms of America's most prestigious ivy-covered universities.

With few exceptions, the growing super wealth and social position of Catholics has not meant a commensurate gain in Catholic institutional life. True, a few Catholic universities can boast large endowments, but even these bear little comparison to America's wealthiest educational institutions. Perceptions to the contrary, the Church is not wealthy. Many Catholic colleges, parochial schools, high schools, parishes, and dioceses — and even a few national Catholic associations — struggle to keep their heads above water.

Within recent times, long rosters of urban parishes and schools in the Northeast, Great Lakes, and Midwest regions of the country have been shuttered and sold. In one year alone, New York City saw 31 of its parishes closed. An epidemic of urban parish school closings is underway, with recent annual totals well exceeding 100.

Few would disagree that the loss of these parishes and schools means a curtailment of the Church's outreach in our cities, especially to the poor. These closings represent a serious contraction of Church ministry and the tragic inability of our dioceses to honor the legacy of thousands of priests, nuns, and working-class laity who labored generously to give these works their start.

In an era of Church scandals, it is tempting to blame parish and school closings on bad management. Yet, long before the sad disclosures of clergy sexual abuse in the Boston Archdiocese and elsewhere, for example, Catholics were showing consistent underperformance as donors. Catholics continue to contribute to their parishes about half of what their Protestant counterparts donate to their own congregations. The typical Catholic parish finds that one out of five parishioners in their pews on Sunday carries the entire financial burden of parish operations.

Fortunately, within the past fifteen years — largely due to a better understanding of the Catholic donor and a pastoral framework set by the U.S. bishops in their letter *Stewardship, A Disciple's Response* — grassroots movements have been taking hold within parishes and dioceses, yielding spectacular results spiritually and financially. Catholics in larger numbers have begun to make the connection between faith and a generous spirit of service and giving.

Research is showing that a deeper sense of participation in Church life is the key to its vitality both spiritually and materially. To bring this about, a new and more vibrant vision of the faith community is required. Clergy, religious, and laity, trusting in God, work together as co-disciples respecting the baptismal equality of one another and share equally in the responsibilities and mission of the faith community. For the Church's institutional leadership, this requires a genuine level of trust in the lay faithful, a spirit of openness and transparency. For the rank-and-file Catholic, this requires a mature faith and a way of life that makes sometimes-painful demands on one's time, talent, and treasure.

It is no accident that Catholicism's expansion and growth in ministry, parish life, education, and service to the poor, right now are found in those areas of the nation that have embraced this stewardship way of life.

This exciting and effective approach to building up the faith community finds encouraging support in several new programs and projects to strengthen church management and to share best practices. An initiative by Dr. Zech at Villanova University has led to the creation of The Center for Church Management, where administrative and managerial training is now available to pastors, as well as parish and diocesan leaders. The new National Leadership Roundtable for Church Management has been launched, bringing together Catholic business and Church leaders to research best practices in financial and human resource management in Catholic institutions. Both are welcome resources as parishes and dioceses look for new ways to strengthen their stewardship.

Within this setting, this publication of the new edition of *Why Catholics Don't Give* is warmly applauded. Dr. Zech's careful research on how Catholics view the Church's handling of money, and his insights on the giving practices of the faithful, offer a concise case for what is needed to achieve a wider and stronger participation of Catholics in the mission of the Church in this ever-challenging environment in which we all seek to serve.

— Dr. Francis J. Butler, President
Foundations and Donors Interested in Catholic Activities, Inc.

FOREWORD TO THE SECOND EDITION

In the six-plus years since *Why Catholics Don't Give... And What Can Be Done About It* was first published, I have been fortunate in being invited to speak on my findings in a number of forums nationwide. These include four presentations at the annual meetings of the International Catholic Stewardship Council, presentations at Diocesan Stewardship Days in eighteen U.S. Catholic Dioceses, and presentations in a handful of parishes. At each forum, I was also afforded the opportunity to mingle with, and learn from, concerned Catholics. These are people who love their Church and are apprehensive about its financial future.

At each of these talks, I was gratified to learn that the basic conclusions contained in the first printing of this book mirrored the experience of these dedicated Catholics. Stewardship is important, they told me, although applied sporadically in our parishes. It is essential to them that they not only know how their contributions are being spent, but also that they have an input into that process. They don't expect to have the final say. They recognize that canon law allocates that responsibility to the pastor. All they ask is to be consulted. They recognize the importance of community building, and the difficulty of accomplishing this in large (and growing) parishes.

Happily, I also learned much from them. The importance of parishioners viewing themselves as involved in ministry — rather than in mere volunteer activities — was a wonderful insight that they gave me. Senior citizens told me of their intention to live out their stewardship in their bequests to the Church. And many are concerned with the willingness of their own children to support the Church at the financial levels of their parents and grandparents.

While the basic findings of the first printing remain, I believe, to be accurate, I have rewritten Chapter 8 ("Seven Things the Catholic Church Can Do to Increase Contributions"). This revised chapter is primarily based on the findings that supported the recommendations contained in the first printing, but they are also embellished by the insights I gathered from my experiences at my presentations.

My education from the presentations was reason enough to require a Second Edition of this book. That requirement seemed even more urgent after the fallout from the clergy sexual abuse scandal. The scandal has dramatic implications for parishioner giving to the Church, both in the short and long terms. I was privileged to be invited by FADICA (Foundations and Donors Interested in Catholic Activities, Inc.) to participate in a series of nationwide surveys that they funded to learn about the attitudes of parishioners in the aftermath of the scandal. The findings from these surveys are reported in a newly written Addendum to this book.

In addition to my good fortune in hearing from parishioners and partnering with FADICA, I have also been blessed to work with the most efficient and effective group of people that I have ever known — the staff at Our Sunday Visitor Press. From the publisher, Greg Erlandson, through the editorial and marketing staffs, I have been regularly impressed by their professionalism and dedication to the Church. Every author should be so lucky as to work with such an impressive group of people.

Finally, it has been my good fate to be associated with a group of knowledgeable scholars who specialize in the social scientific study of the Catholic Church. They are not only smart people, but they are the kind of friends who are willing to mentor me when I'm confused and set me straight when I'm wrong. In the order in which they've entered my professional life, they are: Dean Hoge, Jim Davidson, Thom Jeavons, Patrick McNamara, Michael Donahue, Bob Miller, Michael Cieslak, Jeff Rexhausen, Mary Gautier, and Sr. Mary Bendyna. It is to them that I dedicate this Second Edition.

1

OVERVIEW OF CATHOLIC GIVING

Catholics contribute less money to their churches than do members of nearly every other major U.S. religion. This statement might have raised some eyebrows 20 years ago, but by now it has been firmly supported by mounds of evidence. Study after study has shown Catholics to be less generous to their churches, no matter how that generosity is measured (giving per member, giving per household, giving as a percent of income, etc.).

Just as one example, Figure 1-1 shows how Catholics stack up against other major U.S. religions in giving as a percent of income. The data was collected by Stephen Hart from the General Social Survey for the period 1987-1989. As might be expected, Catholics are well behind the more conservative, evangelical denominations, such as Mormons, who teach tithing as biblically mandated and therefore an integral part of their Christian duty. But Catholics also lag behind the more liberal, mainline Protestant Churches, like Methodists and Presbyterians, whose teachings on the Bible frequently do not differ much from their own. While this data is from the late 1980s, every indication is that this pattern still prevails today.

Fr. Andrew Greeley and Bishop William McManus (1987) were among the first to shed some light on this phenomenon. They looked at Catholic giving over a 25-year period, from 1960 to the mid-1980s, using data from six different surveys. They found an interesting trend. While in the early 1960s Catholics gave approximately the same percent of income to their Church as did mainline Protestants (about 2.2% for both groups), by the late 1970s and through the 1980s, Protestant giving as a percent of income had remained relatively constant at 2.2%, while Catholic giving had been cut in half to about 1.1%.

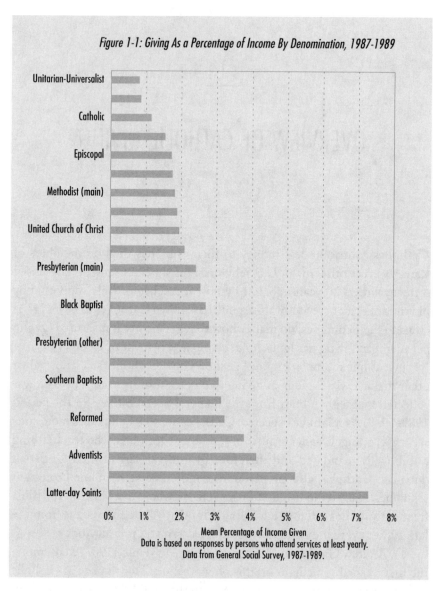

Figure 1-1: Giving As a Percentage of Income By Denomination, 1987-1989

Mean Percentage of Income Given
Data is based on responses by persons who attend services at least yearly.
Data from General Social Survey, 1987-1989.

Subsequent researchers have found a similar pattern, consistently observing that Catholics give at about half the rate of Protestants, although the specific levels of giving differ from study to study. For example, the Independent Sector, a Washington-based coalition of organizations interested in philanthropy and voluntary action, commissioned a series of surveys conducted by the Gallup Organization to provide insights into charitable contributions of both time and money among Americans. While the actual figures differed slightly from year to year because of sampling variation, the pattern of Catholics giving at roughly half the rate of Protestants generally held. For example, figures for 1988 showed Catholics contributing 0.6% of their income to their Church, while Protestants contributed 1.0%; the respective figures for 1990 were 1.3% and 2.4%. Dean Hoge and Fenggang Yang (1994) of Catholic University analyzed data from the 1987-89 General Social Surveys and found Catholics giving 1.2% of their income versus 2.4% for Protestants. Finally, using data from a 1987 survey of 201 congregations (54 Catholic, 147 Protestant) Peter Zaleski and Charles Zech (1994) found Catholic contributions to lag even further behind — $96 per capita versus $297 per person in the Protestant churches.

Unfortunately, because all of these studies use data collected from the mid-1980s or later, none of them have been able to confirm that Catholics at one time gave at the same rate as mainline Protestants and have since slipped, a trend that was so critical to Greeley's and McManus's analysis. But past trends aren't our main concern here. We are interested in the present and the future.

So What?

The low giving of Catholics is not merely of academic interest. It has important ramifications for the Church as it moves into the next millennium. The Church needs all the support it can get to carry out its mission.

Joseph Harris (1994) has estimated that low Catholic giving in the United States costs the Church $1.963 billion a year. That's how much more he estimates that the Church could collect annually if Catholics gave at the average rate for all Americans. Just think what the Church is missing because it doesn't have this $2 billion! Parishes and parish schools have been closed because of financial pressures, many in our inner cities where their presence is most urgent. Maintenance on buildings has been deferred, until it is too late to salvage some otherwise useful facilities. Parishes have been unable to meet the demands of equity as set forth in the U.S. bishops' own pastoral letter, "Economic Justice for All," in paying a fair wage to their staff and parochial schoolteachers. The Church faces huge, unfunded retirement costs for its priests and religious. And of course there is the ongoing work of supporting Catholic social-service agencies in this country, and funding missionaries trying to spread the faith around the world. Sometimes these ramifications have led to dramatic consequences. Joseph Harris (1994) cites the situation in the Chicago Archdiocese, where in 1993 the late Cardinal Bernardin stated, "We will be broke in four years if the Chicago Archdiocese does not address its financial problems immediately." At that point, annual archdiocesan deficits were running in the range of $12 to $15 million a year. Harris goes on to observe that the Chicago situation, while noteworthy because of the vast amounts of money involved, isn't all that unique. He pointed to a study in the *National Catholic Reporter* (Windsor, 1990) that estimated that 10-20% of all U.S. dioceses are operating with a budgetary deficit, while others have already had to make drastic cuts in critical ministries and services in an effort to prevent financial catastrophe.

Everybody Has a Theory

Why is Catholic giving so low? Why do Catholics contribute so much less to their Church than their neighbors who belong to other Christian churches? Are Catholics cheap? Are they less religious? Are they ignorant?

Most researchers who have studied the low level of Catholic giving have felt obliged to offer an explanation. When Fr. Andrew Greeley first showed Bishop McManus how much Catholics lag behind Protestants in their giving, the bishop had a ready answer: Naturally, it's their lower socioeconomic status. Catholics, historically immigrants, have always been below Protestants (and especially mainline Protestants) in their incomes, and low giving is merely a reflection of their lower incomes. Not so, Fr. Greeley informed him. Although this may have been true at one time, Catholics have made great economic strides in the postwar years; today, the annual household income of Catholics is virtually the same as that of mainline Protestants.

Bishop McManus's second explanation concerned the cost of Catholic schools. Parents making the financial sacrifice by paying tuition in order to send their children to parochial schools naturally had less left over to place in the collection basket each Sunday. Again, Fr. Greeley refuted the argument. His figures showed that parents who sent their children to parochial schools actually contributed at higher levels than the average Catholic family. With these two obvious explanations not working, what were the causes?

Greeley's own explanation was controversial. It was alienation, he claimed. The laity were alienated from the Church hierarchy over a number of issues, the most important of which had to do with the Church's teachings on sexual ethics. Church teachings on birth control, which had been widely promulgated in the late 1960s to early 1970s, had angered Catholics. The laity wasn't buying this teaching and was showing its displeasure by withholding contributions.

Bishop McManus held out for another explanation. He felt that Catholics focused too much on their parish's needs (a parish that was out of debt obviously had less need) and not enough on what they themselves could afford to give. He suggested that Catholics be taught to contribute a portion of their income to their Church. Most families, he thought, should be able to contribute two percent of their income, and wealthier households up to four percent.

Other researchers have offered other explanations. Peter Zaleski and Charles Zech (1994), in the study of giving in 201 congregations cited previously, placed most of the blame for low Catholic giving on parish size, focusing their attention on the larger, more impersonal Catholic parishes. In trying to explain the differences in giving between Catholics and Protestants, they asked "what if" Catholics were like Protestants with respect to their socioeconomic status, parish size, and religious attitudes. How would these hypothetical changes impact Catholic giving? They concluded that "reducing Catholic parish size would be the one action having the greatest impact on giving."

In a different study using the same data, Zaleski and Zech (1995) found that Catholic parishes located in regions where Catholics are a minority receive larger contributions than parishes in areas where Catholics constitute a majority of the population. They concluded that parishes that face more competition from other religions are forced to "compete" and are more responsive to parishioners' needs, which in turn results in more generous contributions. Parishes that have a "monopoly" status in that Catholics are the dominant religious group in their region lack these competitive pressures, may be less responsive to parishioners' needs, and thus receive lower contributions.

Like Bishop McManus, John and Sylvia Ronsvale (1995) have focused their analysis on cost differentials between operating a Catholic parish and a Protestant congregation. They've found that in many cases giving follows costs. That is, people give enough to pay the bills. They speculate that the low compensation paid to Catholic clergy, compared to their Protestant counterparts, combined with the larger size of Catholic parishes (more members to support each priest), explains why Catholics give less.

A popular explanation for low Catholic giving emphasizes the laity's dissatisfaction with the amount of participation that they're allowed in church decision-making in general, and with regard to church finances in particular. Frank Butler, director of Foundations and Donors Interested in Catholic Activities (FADICA), was quoted in the 1990 *National Catholic Reporter* article previously cited, and expressed concern over the Church's lack of accountability: "A concern of many Catholics is the clerical control of money and accountability, openness. People are much more willing today to ask questions about how money is being used."

That same article raised another theory for low Catholic giving — the perception that the Church is actually quite wealthy. This is a variation of the arguments made by Bishop McManus and the Ronsvales, that Catholics tie their giving to the costs of running the Church. The article quotes Covington Kern, secretary-treasurer of the Diocesan Fiscal Management Conference: "We don't have some deep, hidden well of cash like Fort Knox. But people perceive that because of (church) buildings."

Fr. Thomas Sweetser (1991), the widely respected founder and co-director of the Parish Evaluation Project, gave his opinion on why Catholic giving is low, based on his consulting experience and surveys. He cited 19 reasons. They included a variation of Greeley's theory of alienation; the belief by many Catholics that the Church really doesn't need the money; and concerns over accountability. But he also added two others. One is the pastor's leadership style, which he argues must be participative and inclusive. The other is that Catholics lack a tradition of planned giving. They are accustomed to giving through weekly offertory collections, and the amounts may depend on how much is available in their checkbook that week. They may not even know how much they've given during the year, or how their giving corresponds to parish expenses.

Jim Castelli (1994), a freelance author who frequently writes on Catholic issues, offered six suggestions for increasing Catholic contributions. They included ideas set forth by others, such as keeping the laity informed on how the money is spent, and the importance of pastors, demonstrating a participative leadership style. He also noted the poor job most seminaries do in training priests in financial management. But he concluded by observing, "When all is said and done, the money crisis facing the Catholic Church is more than a money problem. It's a symptom of larger problems: the decline of community and the confusion about purpose. The way to raise more money for the Church is to become better at being a church."

Msgr. Timothy Collins (1996), a pastor in the Archdiocese of New York, probably articulated the silent belief of many when he expressed the opinion that the problem is church mismanagement, not the lack of money: "Talk to the priests in dioceses where the finances are mismanaged and the structures of the Church neglected. Almost every priest can detail waste and foolishness; many can articulate the hopelessness that such neglect begets."

One approach that has been shown not to increase contributions is the sponsorship of fundraising activities like Bingo. Dean Hoge and Boguslaw Augustyn (1997) examined data collected from 1,682 parishes by the Educational Testing Service as part of its National Survey of Catechists and Religious Education. Among their conclusions were that "use of regular fundraising programs such as Bingo is associated with lower giving. Either the programs themselves, or the parish cultures which underlie such programs, somehow discourage giving" (p. 58).

The U.S. Catholic Bishops had the opportunity to place their mark on the giving issue when they, through the U.S. Catholic Conference, issued a pastoral letter in late 1992 titled "Stewardship: A Disciple's Response." This letter, five years in its development, was expected by many to provide some practical guidance for those in the trenches who are fighting the Church's financial battles. Instead, the bishops opted for a theologically based treatise on the importance of stewardship. They failed to provide any specific recommendations or policies to increase giving. Some praised the bishops for having taken this high road, and for choosing to focus on the total stewardship message of proper use of time, talent, and treasure, rather than just focusing on the money issue. Others expressed frustration that the bishops had ducked the hard questions of putting their theology into practice. They said nothing about better fundraising and increased accountability on their part as to where the money goes.

A Word on Defining Religious Giving

Religious giving can be viewed in essentially two ways. One, a narrow definition, considers contributions made to the parish. These include funds that are meant to support the parish directly, as well as those merely collected by the parish acting as the agent for the larger Church. The former include contributions to support current operations and those that are part of a parish-wide capital campaign. The latter include giving for causes like Catholic Charities, the U.S. Bishops' Campaign for Human Development, and Peter's Pence.

A broader view of religious giving includes any giving resulting from a religious motivation, even if the money is donated to an organization that's not explicitly religious. Examples would include the Red Cross or Habitat for Humanity. Many Catholics contribute to these and similar causes because they believe that it's their Christian duty to support the work of these organizations. Contributions to Catholic colleges and universities would also fit into this category.

This book uses the narrow view of religious giving. It tends to be more precise, since it doesn't require us to speculate on the motive for giving as the broader definition does. We tried to capture a sense of the broader definition when we asked our respondents about their giving to religious and nonreligious groups outside the denomination. Later in this book we examine the extent to which giving to the parish is affected by this broader giving.

Stewardship Versus Fundraising

The study of religious contributions really embraces two separate but related issues. The first is stewardship: returning to God a portion of the bounty that God has given us, making us aware that everything in our life is a gift from God. The second is fundraising: taking care of the financing of the Church as an institution, recognizing that someone has to pay the bills if we want all of the programs and services, both sacramental and nonsacramental, that Catholics believe to be essential components of their religious life. Although there is some tension between the two, both have a legitimate place in the discussion of church finances.

The emphasis on stewardship is relatively recent in the Catholic Church. It's really a post-Vatican II phenomenon. Stewardship stresses motivations for giving, rather than methods. While we can find references to stewardship in the Hebrew Scriptures, it received special emphasis in Jesus' parables. The steward is the household supervisor, responsible to the master for maintaining the master's assets. The analogy, of course, is that we humans don't own the world. God owns the world. We are merely God's servants in maintaining the world. Everything we have comes from God. We are to return a portion of our time, talent, and treasure to God as an expression of our thankfulness for all of God's blessings.

Stewardship is essentially a theological understanding of a total way of life. It is a means for lifting the discussion of money to a spiritual level.

Fundraising, on the other hand, is much more pragmatic. It is concerned with meeting the Church's budgetary requirements. Its message is one of supporting current parish programs and future aspirations. Its focus is on the parish's need to receive, rather than the individual's need to give.

We should be careful not to overstate the differences between stewardship and fundraising. There is a somewhat fuzzy boundary between the two. Many advocates of stewardship are not averse to using the pragmatic tools of fundraisers. Likewise, those whose primary concern is with raising money to support the parish programs they cherish often aren't shy about incorporating the language of stewardship. For example, both might legitimately work at helping parishioners see the connection between raising money to purchase a new organ and their personal relationship with God. In fact, some laity have been known to be cynical about the introduction of stewardship in their parishes, viewing it as just another way of raising money.

In this book we examine both: issues that primarily fall in the realm of stewardship, and those that might more commonly be viewed as fundraising. We also consider other factors affecting giving that probably lie more in the category of "preconditions" necessary for Catholics to respond to either a stewardship or fundraising message.

A Word About Statistics

The results of this study are grounded in sound social-science statistical methodology. Yet, we recognize that most of the readers of this book are not interested in sophisticated statistical methodology. Therefore explanations of the advanced statistics have been omitted. But in the book there are occasional references to some basic statistical concepts. The most important of these is "statistical significance."

Social scientists worry that sometimes the observed relationships between two factors might have occurred by chance, or accident. Before we draw any conclusions, we want to make sure that there is as small a likelihood as possible that the relationship we're observing is accidental. In other words, we want to make sure that the relationship is "significant," that is, not a result of accident or chance, and that it will likely occur again in the future. The criterion that most social scientists use is a 5% or less probability that the relationship they're observing happened by chance. In other words, they're at least 95% certain that it is real and stable, not the result of an accident. There are complex mathematical formulas that allow us to determine the probability that an occurrence is the result of chance. When those formulas indicate that there is less than a 5% probability that the relationship that we've observed is the result of chance, we say the relationship is "statistically significant." The reader can assume that the relationships reported in this book are statistically significant unless we state otherwise.

The Plan of This Book

It's clear from this brief review that observers have suggested a lot of theories trying to explain low Catholic giving and what can be done about it. The purpose of this book is to sort through these theories and opinions and separate the reality from the myths. Unlike the bishops' letter, this book is meant to be practical, not theological. It examines religious giving from a variety of viewpoints, offering recommendations on what can and should be done.

The analysis in this book focuses on data collected for the Lilly Endowment-sponsored American Congregational Giving Study. This was a study of giving in five U.S. denominations: Assemblies of God, Southern Baptists, the Evangelical Lutheran Church of America, Presbyterians, and Roman Catholics. Chapter 2 provides some description of the methodology and general results from that study.

Chapters 3 through 6 examine four types of influences on Catholic religious giving. Personal characteristics of parishioners (age, income, etc.) are considered first, and the impact of each of these characteristics on religious giving is discussed (Chapter 3). Next, we consider how personal religious beliefs of church members influence their giving (Chapter 4). Chapter 5 examines the relationship between denominational policies and programs and parishioners' willingness to contribute. Chapter 6 then considers the effect of parish-level factors on giving.

One of the most interesting phenomena in the Church today is the amount of difference between different generations of Catholics (see Davidson et al., 1997). Studies have shown that young Catholics (the so-called "Generation X") differ dramatically from older Catholics in their beliefs. Earlier studies had shown significant differences between baby-boomers and the generation that had preceded them. Chapter 7 will summarize some of these differences and examine the effect they have on giving patterns across these generations.

The final chapter is titled "Seven Things the Catholic Church Can Do to Increase Contributions." It summarizes the findings of Chapters 3 through 7 and recommends some practical actions that the U.S. Catholic Church should consider if it hopes to increase members' contributions.

References

Castelli, Jim. "Six Ways the Church Can Raise the Money It Needs," *U.S. Catholic*, August, 1994, pp. 6-13.

Collins, Msgr. Timothy S. "Churches, Schools, Survival, and Money: A Pastor Reflects," *Commonweal*, September 13, 1996, pp. 26-28.

Davidson, James D., Andrea S. Williams, Richard A. Lamanna, Jan Stenftenagel, Kathleen Maas Weigert, William J. Whalen, and Patricia Whittberg, S.C. *The Search for Common Ground: What Unites and Divides American Catholics.* Huntington, IN: Our Sunday Visitor Publishing, 1997.

Greeley, Andrew, and William McManus. *Catholic Contributions: Sociology and Policy.* Chicago, IL: Thomas More Press, 1987.

Harris, Joseph Claude. *The Cost of Catholic Parishes and Schools.* Kansas City: Sheed & Ward, 1996.

_____. "U.S. Catholic Contributions — Up or Down?" *America*, May 21, 1994, pp. 14-16.

Hodgkinson, Virginia A., and Murray S. Weitzman. *Giving and Volunteering in the United States: Findings from a National Survey, 1994 Edition.* Washington, DC: Independent Sector.

_____. *Giving and Volunteering in the United States: Findings from a National Survey, 1992 Edition.* Washington, DC: Independent Sector.

_____. *Giving and Volunteering in the United States: Findings from a National Survey, 1990 Edition.* Washington, DC: Independent Sector.

_____. *Giving and Volunteering in the United States: Findings from a National Survey, 1988 Edition.* Washington, DC: Independent Sector.

Hoge, Dean R., and Boguslaw Augustyn. "Financial Contributions to Catholic Parishes: A Nationwide Study of Determinants," *Review of Religious Research*, Vol. 39, No. 1 (September, 1997), pp. 46-60.

Hoge, Dean R., and Fenggang Yang. "Determinants of Religious Giving in American Denominations: Data From Two Nationwide Surveys," *Review of Religious Research*, Vol. 36, No. 2, (December, 1994), pp. 123-148.

Ronsvale, John and Sylvia. *The State of Church Giving Through 1993.* Champaign, IL: empty tomb, inc.,1995.

Sweetser, Thomas P. "The Money Crunch: Why Don't Catholics Give More?" *Chicago Studies*, Vol. 30, No 1 (April, 1991), pp. 99-111.

Windsor, Pat. "Rising Costs, Low Contributions Spell Red Ink for U.S. Dioceses," *National Catholic Reporter*, February 2, 1990, pp. 3-5.

Zaleski, Peter A., and Charles E. Zech. "Economic and Attitudinal Factors in Catholic and Protestant Religious Giving," *Review of Religious Research*, Vol. 36, No. 2 (December 1994), pp. 158-167.

_____. "The Effect of Religious Market Competition on Church Giving," *Review of Social Economy*, Vol. 53, No. 3 (Fall, 1995), pp. 350-367.

2

THE AMERICAN CONGREGATIONAL GIVING STUDY

The Catholic Church is not the only denomination concerned about the financial support that its members are providing. The mainline Protestant churches, in addition to their anxieties over declining membership, are troubled by many of their members' unwillingness to pledge. Evangelical Protestants, who teach the tithe as an integral part of their religious doctrine, worry because many of their members are not tithers. It seems that no church is entirely satisfied with the financial support that it receives from its members. For this reason, the Lilly Endowment of Indianapolis, Indiana, in late 1992 commissioned a nationwide study of giving in U.S. churches, which came to be known as The American Congregational Giving Study. Four researchers were enlisted to undertake this study. Dean Hoge, a Presbyterian layman and a sociologist at Catholic University, led the team. He was joined by Michael Donahue, a psychologist who at that time was employed by Search Institute, a Minneapolis-based consulting firm; Patrick McNamara, also a sociologist, from the University of New Mexico; and Charles Zech, an economist from Villanova University.

In early 1993, the research team set about conducting a nationwide survey of U.S. churches and church members in order to learn more about religious giving. Their efforts culminated in a book, *Money Matters: Personal Giving in American Churches*, which was published by Westminster/John Knox Press in 1996. That book was primarily concerned with learning about the basic factors influencing religious giving in general. This book uses the data collected for that study, and the lessons learned from it, to analyze religious giving only in the Catholic Church.

How the American Congregational Giving Study Was Done

The research team focused its attention on five U.S. religious denominations. Along with the Catholic Church, two relatively high-giving evangelical churches, the Assemblies of God and the Southern Baptist Convention, were included in the study. Two medium-giving mainline Protestant denominations, the Presbyterian Church and the Evangelical Lutheran Church of America, were also selected.

The team decided to study 125 parishes in each denomination, chosen across the nine U.S. census regions. Church membership is uneven, with many small parishes and a few large ones in each denomination. Whereas most parishes are small, most members belong to the large ones. For this reason, the team elected to oversample large parishes, with half of the sample coming from the largest third of the parishes in the region. Otherwise, the sample of churches was random, and was selected by team members, not by denominational officials. Later the bias caused by oversampling the larger parishes was removed by weighting the data.

Field workers personally visited each parish in the sample. Most of the field workers were retired or part-time clergy, or retired church officials. They had two tasks. First, they assisted the pastor (or on occasion, a parish staff member) in the completion of a Congregational Profile (see Appendix A), which summarized the member socioeconomic characteristics, beliefs, and programs in the parish. Second, they (not the pastor or staff person) selected a random sample of 30 parish members. Each of these was sent a lay questionnaire, which asked members about their personal beliefs, opinions about both the parish and the denomination, and their personal socioeconomic characteristics (Appendix B). The lay questionnaires were returned directly to the research team, not to the pastor. Overall, 61.2% of the lay questionnaires were returned. The response rate was 55.2% for the Assemblies of God, 53.9% among Southern Baptists, 66.7% for Presbyterians, 70.1% for Lutherans, and 60.5% for Catholics. Because 30 members were surveyed from each parish, regardless of size, a second weighting took place to ensure an appropriate distribution of church members in the sample.

Like most studies of this kind, the individuals who returned the lay questionnaires were not totally representative of the overall church membership. They tended to be more urban, more highly educated, with higher incomes, and more committed to their church, than typical church members. Again, this is common, but any analysis of the lay questionnaires should keep this in mind. Likewise, a few members reported making huge contributions to their church in the last year. Not many households can afford to give $25,000 or more to their church on an annual basis, but some members of our sample did. These were most likely one-time gifts, and not indicative of overall giving patterns. Social scientists typically drop these "outliers" from the sample, if there aren't too many of them, and that's what we did.

As a check on its sampling, the research team also commissioned a Gallup telephone survey of U.S. church members. Because of the difficulty in collecting an adequate sample from the smaller denominations in the study, the Gallup survey included only people who said they were Baptists, Lutherans, or Catholics. The Gallup survey asked the same questions that had been asked on the lay questionnaire, except that it also included questions on matters of sexual ethics that Andrew Greeley had found to be so important in explaining the decline in Catholic contributions.

Finally, after all of the data had been collected, the researchers interviewed a number of pastors and lay leaders. These interviews resulted in a variety of quotes that were rich in insights and understanding of Church and put a human face on the raw data.

Description of the Parishes in the Sample

What did the Catholic parishes look like? How were they different from the Protestant churches? Remember, these are the characteristics of the parishes as a whole, not of the sample of members who completed the lay questionnaire.

Size and Age Characteristics of the Parishes

Figures 2-1 through 2-3 summarize some of the descriptive characteristics of the churches in our sample. They show that Catholic parishes in our sample tended to be about middle-aged, compared to the mainline Protestant churches, which are older, and the evangelical churches, which

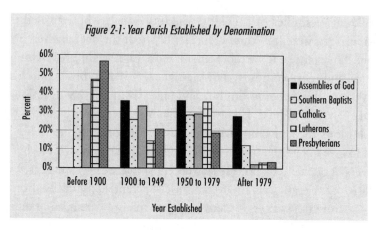

Figure 2-1: Year Parish Established by Denomination

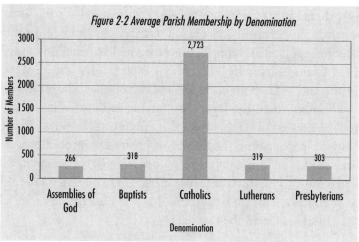

Figure 2-2 Average Parish Membership by Denomination

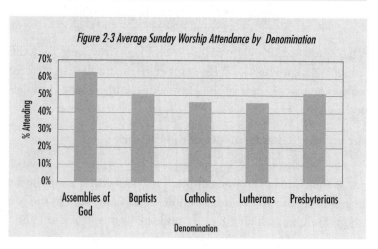

Figure 2-3 Average Sunday Worship Attendance by Denomination

are younger. Catholic parishes were by far the largest (almost eight times larger than the average Protestant church in our sample). Surprisingly, in spite of the Catholic Church's historic emphasis on Sunday Mass attendance, Catholic parishes had the second lowest percent of their members attending weekly services, barely edging out the Lutherans.

Parish Members' Characteristics

Figures 2-4 through 2-8 summarize the member demographic characteristics of the parishes in our sample. The Catholic parishes were similar to the Protestant congregations in their gender distribution and were about in the middle in the age distribution of their members. Like the

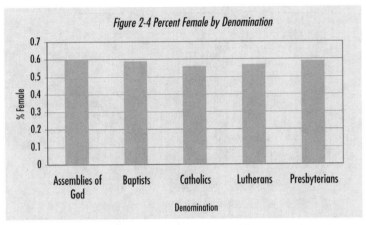

Figure 2-4 Percent Female by Denomination

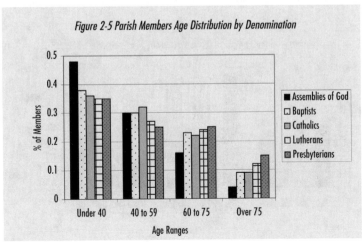

Figure 2-5 Parish Members Age Distribution by Denomination

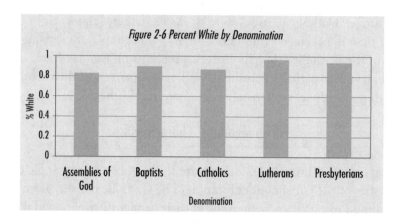

Figure 2-6 Percent White by Denomination

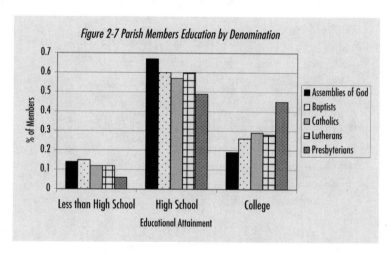

Figure 2-7 Parish Members Education by Denomination

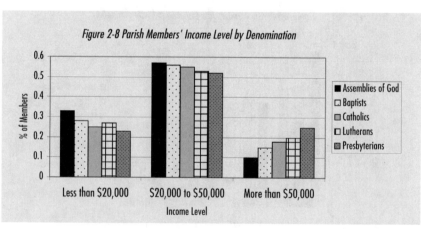

Figure 2-8 Parish Members' Income Level by Denomination

Protestant parishes in the sample, the Catholic parishes were overwhelmingly white. Neither the education distribution nor the income distribution of the members of the Catholic parishes in our sample differed remarkably from those of the sample's Protestant congregations.

Parish Finances

The receipts that the parishes in the sample received from various sources are shown in Figures 2-9 through 2-11. As one might expect, Catholic parishes, since they're much larger than the Protestant parishes in our sample, had the largest amount of total receipts. But, as Figure 2-10 demonstrates, next to Presbyterians, Catholics were least likely to rely on regular offerings to support their church. The remainder of their budget was met by heavy reliance on special offerings, fundraisers (Bingo?), and a variety of other sources, including income earned from investments and income generated by renting out parish facilities. Figure 2-11 shows, just as every other study on the topic has shown, that Catholic parishioners in our sample contributed far less to their church than did the Protestants in our sample.

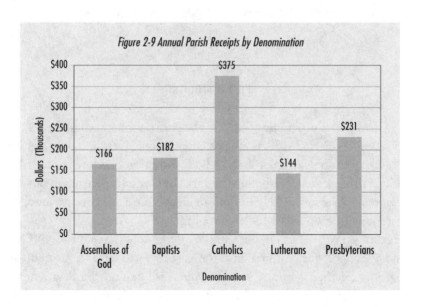

Figure 2-9 Annual Parish Receipts by Denomination

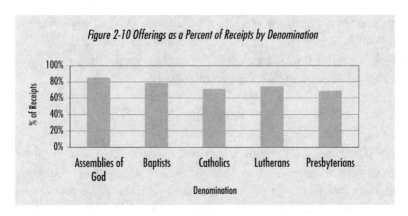

Figure 2-10 Offerings as a Percent of Receipts by Denomination

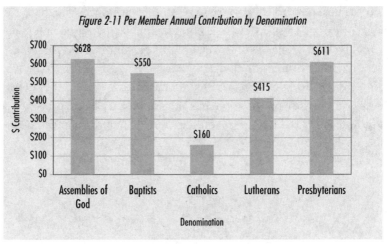

Figure 2-11 Per Member Annual Contribution by Denomination

Parish Programs

The types of programs offered in the parishes in our sample are shown in Figures 2-12 to 2-15. As might be expected, Catholic parishes were more likely to sponsor a parochial school, either on their own or in collaboration with another parish. Surprisingly, the Catholic parishes in our sample were also the most likely to sponsor a day-care center or preschool, and most likely to sponsor a latchkey program.

Almost every parish in our sample offered religious education (CCD, Sunday School) for children, and the vast majority also sponsored these programs for their youth. Catholics were well behind the Protestants in our sample in their offering of adult religious education. Catholics also

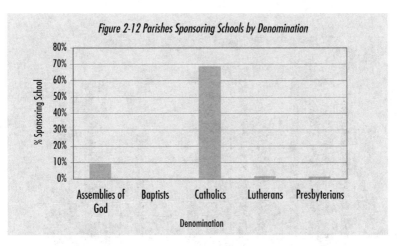

Figure 2-12 Parishes Sponsoring Schools by Denomination

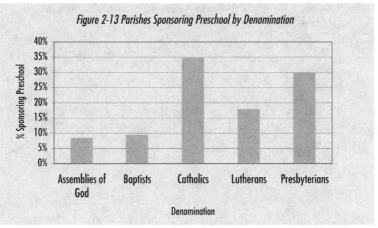

Figure 2-13 Parishes Sponsoring Preschool by Denomination

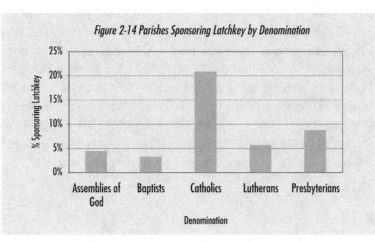

Figure 2-14 Parishes Sponsoring Latchkey by Denomination

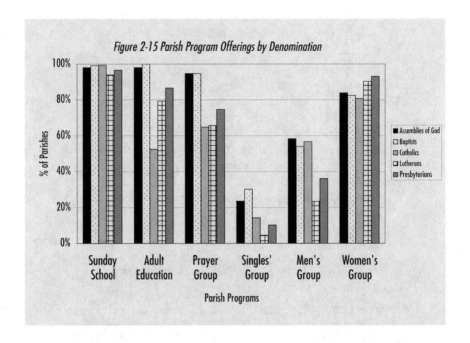

Figure 2-15 Parish Program Offerings by Denomination

tended to lag behind in their offering of prayer or study groups, but they were comparable to the Protestants in the sample in their offerings of adult special-interest groups, providing more of some, but less of others.

Summary

This chapter has provided a brief summary of the American Congregational Giving Study and a description of the sample of parishes that comprised the study. The rest of this book is concerned with our findings from investigating the Catholic parishes and laity in our sample. But from time to time, to put our findings in perspective, they will be compared to the Protestants that we studied. Oftentimes the Catholics in our sample give their Church a lower rating on issues of concern than do the Protestants. Where this occurs, we simply point it out. We leave it to the reader to decide if a low rating in some categories is truly warranted, and whether in each particular case a low rating is a good thing or a bad thing.

References

Dean R. Hoge, Charles E. Zech, Patrick McNamara, and Michael J. Donahue. *Money Matters: Personal Giving in American Churches.* Louisville: Westminster/John Knox, 1996.

Readers interested in a more thorough explanation of methodology involved in collecting the data for this study should consult: Dean R. Hoge, Charles E. Zech, Patrick McNamara, and Michael J. Donahue. *Research Report on the American Congregational Giving Study*, Life Cycle Institute, The Catholic University of America, 1995. The Report can be found in the libraries of Catholic University, The University of New Mexico, and Villanova University.

3

PERSONAL PARISHIONER CHARACTERISTICS

This brief chapter considers myths and realities concerning the effect of parishioners' personal characteristics on their religious giving. How do people's income level, age, race, and so on affect their contributions to the Church? It could be concluded that these factors, while of interest, are really outside of the Church's control and therefore carry no policy implications. On the other hand, to the extent that the Church can target its message and programs, it's important that it knows about the giving patterns of people with different personal characteristics. For example, if it can be shown that people with high incomes have a different giving pattern than other parishioners, or respond to different giving messages, then a parish with a large number of high earners should be able to take advantage of that information to target that group. The same may be true for a parish with a large number of unmarried members, or a parish with a substantial minority population, and so on. This chapter investigates the giving levels associated with various personal characteristics.

There is a close relationship between people's personal characteristics and their income. A household's income level is so important that it overshadows the effects of other characteristics on its contributions. In recognition of this problem, this chapter views religious contributions both from the perspective of the dollar amounts and the percent of household income that is contributed.

Income

Every study has found income to be an important factor in explaining people's religious contributions. Basically, dollar contributions increase as people's incomes rise. Households with more income can afford to contribute more. Our data agrees with this pattern. Figure 3-1 divides our sample into six income-categories. Households in higher income categories contribute more. The only exception is a blip among middle-income classifications, where households in the $35,000- to $50,000-income range contribute more than those earning $50,000 to $75,000. But the overall pattern is apparent.

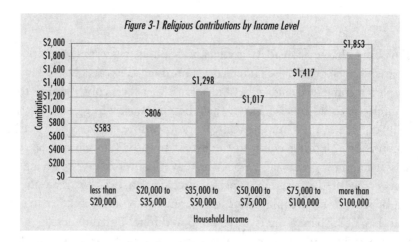

Figure 3-1 Religious Contributions by Income Level

Households with more income contribute more to the Church. But does the increase in contributions increase at the same rate as income? Does one household that earns twice as much income as another household contribute twice as much? Most of the research on this question has concluded that the answer is no. Contributions increase as household incomes increase, but at a slower rate. Upper-income households contribute more dollars than do lower-income households, but they contribute a lower *percentage* of their income. Our findings are shown in Figure 3-2, where we compare the percentage of income contributed across the six income categories. Here we see a generally decreasing pattern (again with that blip among lower-middle-income households).

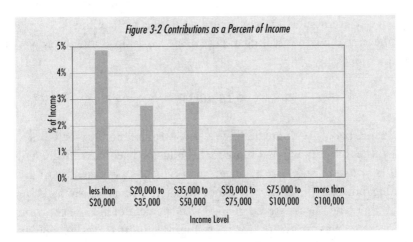

Figure 3-2 Contributions as a Percent of Income

Higher-income households contribute far less, as a portion of their income, than do lower-income households. In fact, those households earning more than $100,000 contribute only about one-fourth as much of their income as those earning less than $20,000.

In *Money Matters* we found a similar pattern for the Protestants in our sample. Higher-income Protestants also gave a lower percent of their income. But the decrease wasn't as dramatic as it was for Catholics. There are generally two explanations set forth to account for this pattern. One is that households view their contributions to the Church as containing two elements. The first component is to pay their "fair share" of parish membership. This figure would be a constant dollar figure for all households, regardless of their income. The second element contains a "proportion of income" component, whereby people recognize that wealthier households should contribute a proportionately larger share of their income. Combining these two elements results in the observed pattern: as a household's income increases, dollar contributions increase (because of the proportion of income component) but not at the same rate as income has increased (because the fixed, fair-share component has not changed).

The other explanation is that households base their contributions on the level of income that they *expect* to receive in a particular time period. Sometimes their expectations are wrong, and they actually earn more money than they thought they would. But none of this unanticipated increase in income is contributed to the Church, so if their income has unexpectedly increased, contributions as a percent of income will decrease.

In any event, all churches, including the Catholic Church, have a big job ahead of them in instilling a sense of stewardship among their wealthiest members.

Education

Just as people with greater incomes contribute more to the Church, so too, studies have shown that more highly educated people contribute more. This is not surprising, since education is typically associated with greater earning power. However, when looking at the *trend* in giving, Greeley found that when he measured giving by the percent of income contributed, the decrease was far greater for more highly educated Catholics than for those with less education. From 1963 to 1984, contributions as a percent of income decreased from 2.4% to 1.3% for those who went to college, compared to a decrease from 2.0% to 1.3% for those who did not graduate from high school. Greeley attributed this sharper decline among more educated Catholics to their greater dissatisfaction with the Church's authoritarian structure and moral stances (Greeley and McManus, 1987, pp. 40-41, 44).

Our data did not allow the identification of any trends. But, as Figure 3-3 shows, Catholics with more education contributed more.

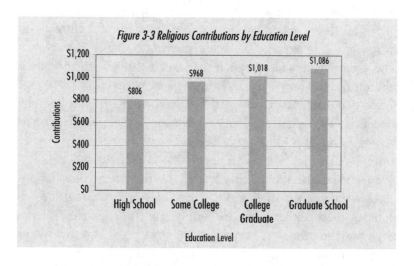

Figure 3-3 Religious Contributions by Education Level

At the same time our results support Greeley's contention that more highly educated Catholics contribute a lower percentage of their income. Figure 3-4 shows that on a percent-of-income basis Catholics with a college degree or more contribute only about two-thirds as much as those without a college degree. The premise that this pattern is caused by greater dissatisfaction with the denomination is tested later in this book. But we can note here that the findings are inconclusive.

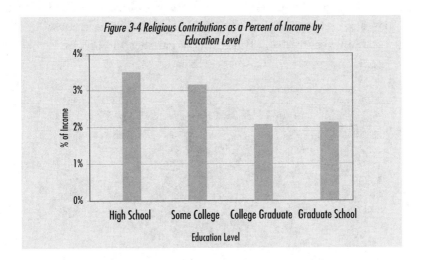

Figure 3-4 Religious Contributions as a Percent of Income by Education Level

Race

Most studies have shown that whites contribute more to their churches than do racial minorities. This has been partially attributed to their generally higher levels of income. So as with other personal characteristics, the analysis of giving patterns by race must consider both actual dollars contributed as well as the percent of income.

We found no difference at all in the dollar contributions between whites and non-whites (there were too few non-whites in our sample to allow for a more detailed breakdown of racial minorities). Likewise, there was no significant difference between them when giving was measured by the percent of income. For Catholics, minorities do not contribute at any different levels than do whites. In *Money Matters* we found a similar pattern for the Protestant denominations that we studied. Race is apparently not a consideration in determining religious contributions.

Family Status

Researchers all agree that married people contribute more than do single, separated, widowed, or divorced church members. Several reasons have been suggested. One is that it may be the result of higher incomes for married couples, many of which are two-income families. Another explanation is that churches don't do an adequate job in getting their unmarried members involved. Most churches offer a variety of programs for children, such as a parochial school or CCD, CYO, youth choirs, Scout troops, etc. Parents naturally get involved. But in many parishes the program offerings that appeal to unmarried members are sparse.

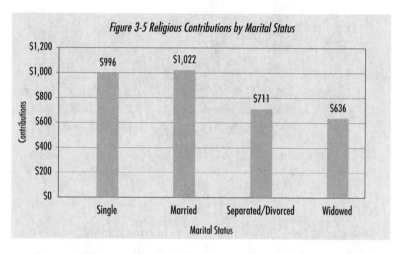

Figure 3-5 Religious Contributions by Marital Status

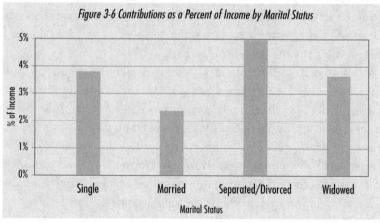

Figure 3-6 Contributions as a Percent of Income by Marital Status

In Figure 3-5 we can see that married households contribute significantly more than do widowed and separated/divorced Catholics, but only slightly more than single parishioners. But from Figure 3-6 we can see that this is partially a result of these households' higher incomes. Based on the percentage of their income contributed, married couples contribute significantly *less* than do other parish households.

Apart from income, does the existence of children in a family make a difference? What about the myth that because many parish programs are geared toward children, having children in the home leads to more attachment to the parish, and thus larger contributions? The answer here is mixed. From Figure 3-7 we can conclude that households with two or

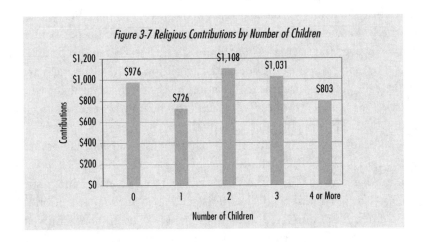

Figure 3-7 Religious Contributions by Number of Children

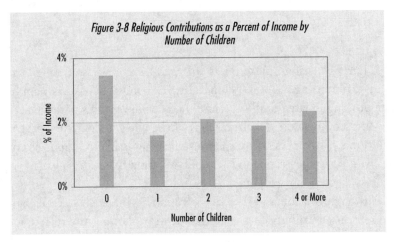

Figure 3-8 Religious Contributions as a Percent of Income by Number of Children

three children under the age of 18 living at home contribute more than do other households. But smaller families (one child at home) and larger families (four or more children at home) contribute less than do families with no children living at home. And Figure 3-8 reveals that households with no children contribute a larger portion of their income to the Church. So the reality is that higher incomes — rather than parish attachment brought about by their children's participation — explains the higher giving levels of married households.

What about the religious preference of a spouse? Do households where both the husband and wife are Catholics contribute more than a household where one of the parties is not a Catholic? One would probably think so, if attachment to the parish is enhanced by both partners sharing the same faith. But the reality is that it doesn't make any difference. We found that married households where both partners are Catholic do not contribute more (in fact, they actually contribute slightly less) than do households where one of the spouses is not Catholic, although the differences are not statistically significant. One explanation might be that Catholics who are married to non-Catholics (who tend to be more generous to their churches) are positively influenced by the example of their spouses.

Some of the family variables (such as being married) are associated with higher religious contributions. The impact of others (such as having children) is erratic. They show no clear pattern of either increasing or decreasing contributions. Still others (such as if one's spouse attends the same church) are unrelated to church giving. At best, then, family status would be considered a weak determinant of religious giving.

Age

A fairly consistent pattern has emerged from studies on religious giving by different age groups. Generally, contributions rise as people get older, peaking in late middle age, and then declining. This pattern has been shown to prevail across denominations. As people get older, they have more discretionary income that they can use for things like religious contributions. But once they retire and begin living on a fixed income, they again have less discretionary income.

Although the ebb and flow of discretionary income as people age has no doubt historically been a main factor in explaining the differences in giving by age, recent research has focused on generational differences (see Davidson et al., 1997). According to this theory, the defining moment for Catholics was Vatican II. The Catholic Church today, then, is really composed of three generations: the pre-Vatican II generation; the Vatican II generation; and the post-Vatican II generation. Catholics who came of age prior to Vatican II (essentially those born before and during WWII) were raised in a hierarchical church, where the emphasis was on tradition. When they speak of the Church, they are most likely referring to the magisterium. They tend to regard the Church as an institution, and are more likely to support it financially.

The post-Vatican II generation consists of those who came of age after Vatican II had occurred and most of its reforms had been implemented. They were raised in a Church with a decreased emphasis on tradition and an increased emphasis on democratic processes and the primacy of individual conscience. When they think of the Church, they think of it in terms of "the people of God." They have less of an institutional commitment to the Church, and are more reluctant to support it financially.

The Vatican II generation primarily encompasses the baby-boomer generation, especially those born before 1960. They are caught in the middle. They came of age during Vatican II and the transition period that followed it. They have one foot in the old church and one foot in the new. Although they may continue some of the devotional practices of the Church that are dear to the hearts of the pre-Vatican II generation, in most attitudes they tend to be more like post-Vatican II Catholics. This includes their attitude toward financial support of the Church.

The impact of these generational differences as possible explanations for any differences in religious contributions are discussed in Chapter 7. For now, we can recognize that there are differences in giving among these different generations, and the differences reflect the pattern discussed at the beginning of this section. As Figure 3-9 illustrates, religious contributions increase as one moves from the youngest group through the late middle-age group, and then they decline for those 65 or older. Contributions as a percent of income increase uniformly as one moves from the youngest to the oldest age brackets (Figure 3-10). This reality is consistent with the myth that the effect of age on religious contributions depends on the availability of discretionary income during each of the periods of a person's life.

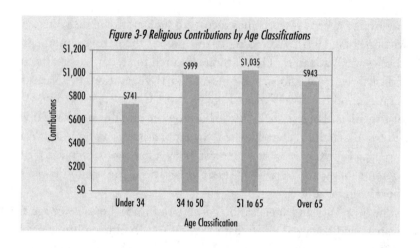

Figure 3-9 Religious Contributions by Age Classifications

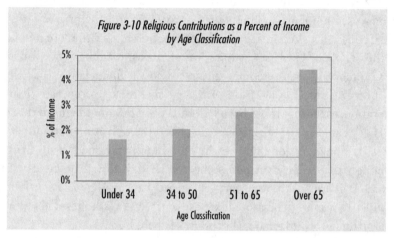

Figure 3-10 Religious Contributions as a Percent of Income by Age Classification

Philanthropy Outside the Parish

We have frequently heard it said that one reason that Catholic giving lags behind that of other denominations is because Catholics are so generous in giving to causes outside their parishes. These include donations to their colleges, religiously based organizations like Catholic Charities, and secular causes such as the United Way. But this is a myth that cannot be supported in reality.

For one thing, in *Money Matters* we found that Catholics in our sample donated an average of $576 per household to religious and non-religious causes outside their parish. This was the second lowest among the five denominations. Presbyterians were the most generous, contributing an average of $816 per household. Members of the Assembly of God gave an average of $716, Southern Baptists donated $615, and Lutherans contributed an average of $526 to organizations outside their congregation.

A second reason why this myth can't be supported is that those Catholics who are the most generous in their contributions to causes outside the parish are *also* the largest contributors to their parish. Figure 3-11 shows that Catholics who donate more to organizations outside the parish also contribute more to their parish. This does not support the existence of any trade-off in the minds of Catholics between giving to their parish and donating to other causes. Rather, it shows that whatever generosity exists among Catholics extends to both their parish and to other worthwhile causes. The tendency to be generous to one's parish is closely related to generosity to other charitable causes.

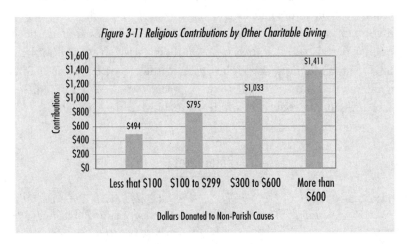

Figure 3-11 Religious Contributions by Other Charitable Giving

Although the differences are not statistically significant, it should be mentioned that when contributions to the parish are measured as a percent of income, the relationship is just the reverse: Catholics' contributions to their parish as a percent of their income decrease when they donate more to other organizations.

So, contrary to the unfounded myth, we can conclude that low Catholic giving to their churches has nothing to do with generosity to other charitable organizations.

Conclusions

From this brief review of the effect of various personal characteristics on Catholic contributions, we found two that were strongly related to religious contributions. One, as we had expected, was income. Not only was income itself found to significantly affect religious contributions, but, with few exceptions (race being one notable case), personal characteristics that tend to be associated with higher incomes were also associated with higher levels of religious contributions. But while this was the finding when we considered the dollar amounts contributed, the reverse was generally true when we examined the portion of people's incomes that they contributed. High-income households (and people with characteristics associated with higher incomes) gave a lower percentage of their incomes to the Church.

The other strong relationship that we found was between people's donations to charitable causes and organizations outside the parish and their contributions to the parish. Households with larger contributions to other charities also contributed more to their parish. It would not be reasonable to argue that one *causes* the other. Rather, some of the same underlying factors that induce people to be generous in their other philanthropy are also influencing their decision to contribute to the Church.

References

Davidson, James D. et al. *The Search for Common Ground: What Unites and Divides Catholic Americans.* Huntington, IN: Our Sunday Visitor Publishing, 1997.

Greeley, Andrew, and William McManus. *Catholic Contributions: Sociology and Policy.* Chicago: The Thomas More Press, 1987.

Hoge, Dean R., Charles E. Zech, Patrick McNamara, and Michael J. Donahue. *Money Matters: Personal Giving in American Churches,* Louisville: Westminster/John Knox, 1996.

4

RELIGIOUS BELIEFS
AND COMMITMENT

In the previous chapter, we considered the effect of socioeconomic factors on Catholic religious giving. We observed that though the impact of these factors on giving is important to understand, they are generally beyond the Church's control. The best the Church can hope to do is to recognize that different parishioners — for example, unmarried parishioners — have different pastoral needs that must be met. Meeting those needs will result in greater satisfaction with the Church. One by-product of this may well be that these members will increase their religious contributions.

This chapter carries a similar theme, in that it examines the effect on giving of factors that the Church is either unwilling or unable to change, but whose effect on giving can serve as a valuable pastoral signal. It is important for the Church to understand the effect of both people's religious beliefs and commitment on their contributions. Not because it would want to change its teachings merely to attract more contributions, but rather because understanding the impact that its teachings may be having on contributions will help the Church to respond pastorally. For example, if Andrew Greeley is correct, and a major reason for low Catholic contributions is alienation over the Church's teaching on issues like birth control, this is important information. It would signal the Church that it hasn't done an adequate job pastorally in explaining its position. Without information like this, the Church may come to believe that everything is fine, and continue on the same path without addressing underlying problems.

This chapter first looks at the impact that some beliefs have on Catholic contributions. Later, we consider the effect of religious commitment on contributions. Are the more religiously committed contributing more, as we would expect? If they're not, we have even a more challenging task ahead of us if we hope to increase Catholic contributions.

Beliefs

Other than Greeley, not many researchers have considered the effect of specific religious beliefs on giving, perhaps because they've concluded that churches are unwilling to modify their teachings merely to attract larger contributions. Those few studies that have looked at the effect of beliefs have always concluded that parishioners with more orthodox beliefs and more conservative attitudes on moral issues contribute more. For example, John Hilke (1980) compared the effect of religious orthodoxy on contributions across a number of Protestant denominations. He found it to have a strong effect on religious giving. Andrew Greeley, in another study that he coauthored with William McCready and Kathleen McCourt (1976), found a moderate relationship between contributions and both people's agreement with Church teachings and their reluctance to criticize priests. Dean Hoge and Fenggang Yang (1994) found that Catholics who do the following tended to be more generous givers: those who prayed more often, believed in life after death, considered the Bible to be an important guide in making life decisions, regard Church teaching as being an important guide in making life decisions, believe their faith to be free of doubts, and consider premarital sex to be always wrong. Another study, by D'Antonio et al. (1989), reported that Catholics who agreed with the Church's position on artificial contraception, abortion, and punishment of dissenting theologians, contributed more. But those who approved of some of the Church's more liberal positions, such as the Bishops' letters on the nuclear-arms race and the economy, and the notion of the preferential option for the poor, also gave more. D'Antonio et al. also looked at the effect of attitudes about Church authority on contributions. They found that parishioners who agree that Church leaders should have the final say on what is morally right or wrong regarding both abortion and birth control contributed more than did others. Those who thought these should be joint decisions between the leadership and members gave the next most.

The lowest givers were those who felt that abortion and birth control should be individual decisions.

We can conclude from all of this that it is the willingness to accept the Church's official position, and the acknowledgement of its teaching authority, as much as the Church's stance on any one specific issue, that motivates people to contribute more.

In this chapter we consider some beliefs for which the Church may not have taken an official position.

Distinctive Lifestyle Teachings

Researchers who have compared giving patterns across denominations have found higher contributions in so-called "high-tension" churches (Iannaccone, 1994). These are churches that impose demands on their members, such as abstinence from alcohol or certain types of entertainment like movies or dancing, which set them apart from the rest of society. We found this to be true in *Money Matters*. Denominations that place demands on their members that cause them to live a distinctive lifestyle, such as the Assemblies of God and the Southern Baptists, received greater contributions from their members. But this was not true for the Catholic Church. While the Church does not encourage activities such as drinking and gambling, it does not outlaw them, so long as they're done in moderation. But some individual pastors do take a harder line on these activities. Do these "high-tension parishes" receive larger contributions? No. Contributions in parishes that claimed to place a special emphasis on teaching abstinence from common societal experiences did not vary significantly from parishes that did not make these demands.

Christian Duty

What about uniquely Christian beliefs? We asked our lay respondents if it is true that only followers of Jesus Christ can be saved. At one time this was a teaching of the Catholic Church. Since Vatican II the Church has backed off this position. Yet 52% of our sample of lay Catholics either agreed with this statement or were uncertain. However, as Figure 4-1 shows, those who disagreed contribute substantially more than the other two groups.

Figure 4-1 Religious Contributions by "Only Followers of Jesus Can Be Saved"

We asked our respondents what they believe to be the primary duty of Christians. Over 60% chose the option, "Following the teachings of Jesus as the basis for spiritual growth." But, as Figure 4-2 illustrates, these were the *lowest givers*. The highest givers were those who responded, "Faithfully participating in the tradition and sacraments of the Church" (22% of the sample) and those (6% of the sample) who selected, "Helping to change unjust social structures." Another 6% chose the response frequently identified with evangelical Christians, "Helping others commit their lives to Christ." This outcome is perplexing. When we think of orthodox beliefs in the Catholic Church, we tend to reflect, as did our sample, on tradition and sacraments, and the importance of Jesus. Yet one of these is associated with high contributions, while the other results in low contributions. A small

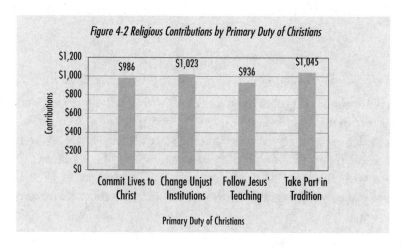

Figure 4-2 Religious Contributions by Primary Duty of Christians

minority of our respondents believes that their primary duty is to change unjust social structures, an issue that has received relatively less emphasis by the Church. But they are among the better givers. Perhaps these results reflect confusion on the part of parishioners concerning the Church's post-Vatican II message.

Religion in Daily Life

We asked parishioners about the role that religion plays in their daily lives. Almost two-thirds agreed with the statement, "What religion offers me most is comfort in times of trouble and sorrow." But their giving was not significantly different from those who disagreed with that statement or were uncertain. On the other hand, those three-fourths of the respondents who agreed with the statement, "My whole approach to life is based on my religion," contributed significantly more than those who disagreed or were uncertain (Figure 4-3). This is good news for those who make the argument that stewardship, including its financial component, is an essential part of Christian living.

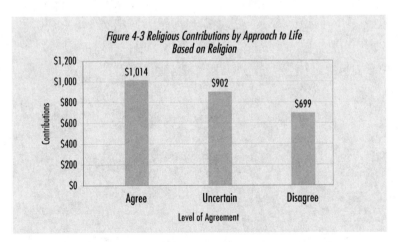

Figure 4-3 Religious Contributions by Approach to Life Based on Religion

Sexual Ethics

What about Andrew Greeley's contention that it is alienation with the Church's hierarchy over teachings on sexual ethics that is the primary culprit in explaining low Catholic giving? In addition to our congregation profiles and lay survey, we had also contracted with the Gallup Organization to conduct a nationwide survey of church members, including 535 Catholics. Household religious contributions were lower in the Gallup sample than they were in the lay-survey sample. In our Gallup poll we asked about Church teachings on abortion, birth control, and the ordination of women. The sample tended to agree with the Church's position on abortion (54%) and the ordination of women (56%), but disagree with its position on birth control (only 39% agreed). Except for the ordination of women, those who agreed with the Church's position contributed more than those who disagreed or were uncertain, but the differences were not significantly different (Figures 4-4 to 4-6). This finding is consistent with Greeley's hypothesis that parishioners who are angry with the Church over

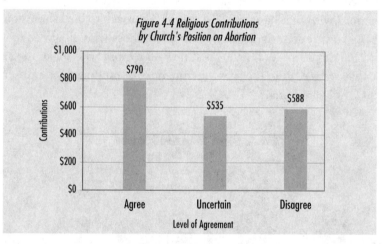

Figure 4-4 Religious Contributions by Church's Position on Abortion

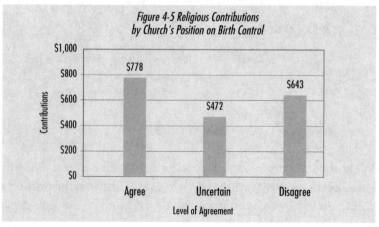

Figure 4-5 Religious Contributions by Church's Position on Birth Control

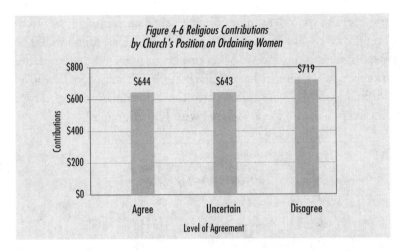

Figure 4-6 Religious Contributions by Church's Position on Ordaining Women

some of its sexual-ethics teachings are giving less. But the relationship is weak; it comes nowhere close to supporting his contention that this dissatisfaction is the *primary* explanation for low Catholic giving.

Commitment

Every study of religious giving has found a strong relationship between assorted measures of religious commitment and contributions. This is not to imply that various forms of religious commitment, like Mass attendance or volunteering to serve on parish committees, *cause* parishioners to contribute more. Rather, it is probably an indication that contributing toward the support of their church is simply another way that members play out their religious commitment. The same feelings about their church that induce parishioners to attend daily Mass or volunteer to help clean up the church grounds will probably also cause them to be more generous in supporting their church financially.

Commitment to the Denomination

When we think of religious commitment, we usually think in terms of commitment to the parish, where the opportunities to demonstrate that commitment are more readily available. Yet, on many criteria, including their reluctance to change religions, Catholics are more committed to their denomination than are most other Christians. We had one measure of their commitment to their denomination. We asked our sample how often they read publications (magazines, newspapers, and newsletters) published by the denomination or diocese. Most of our sample read denominationally sponsored publications either regularly (36%) or occasionally (36%). As shown in Figure 4-7, commitment to the denomination as measured by reading its publications is associated with higher giving.

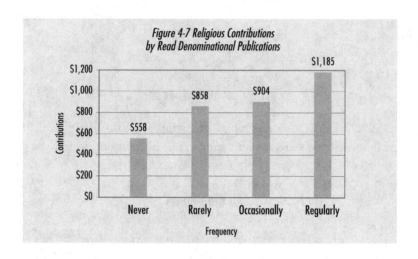

Figure 4-7 Religious Contributions by Read Denominational Publications

Commitment to the Parish

We had a variety of measures of commitment to the parish, all of which were significantly related to higher giving. We asked people how long they had been members of their parish (Figure 4-8). Generally, the longer they had been parishioners, the more they gave. Curiously, this was not true at the extremes. New parishioners gave more, and the most senior parishioners gave less, than the overall pattern would have predicted. Low giving on the part of the most senior parishioners might be explained by observing that many of them are probably retired and living on a fixed income, as we discussed in Chapter 3. It's more difficult to understand the high giving on the part of new parishioners. This may be a statistical aberration, since new parishioners made up a small portion of our sample (about 2%). With such a small number of respondents, even one exceptionally large giver in this group could have inflated the average.

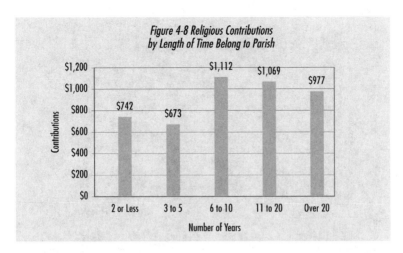

Figure 4-8 Religious Contributions by Length of Time Belong to Parish

What about Mass attendance? Predictably those who attend more frequently also contribute more (Figure 4-9). Likewise, those who attend more non-worship events at their parish also are more generous contributors (Figure 4-10).

In the previous chapter we addressed the myth that one reason Catholics are such poor contributors to their parishes is that they are so generous in supporting other causes. We found that this myth couldn't be supported. Catholics who are more generous to other causes are also more generous to their churches. Another myth is that Catholics perceive a trade-off among the stewardship components of time, talent, and treasure. We've had plenty of church members tell us about cases where their

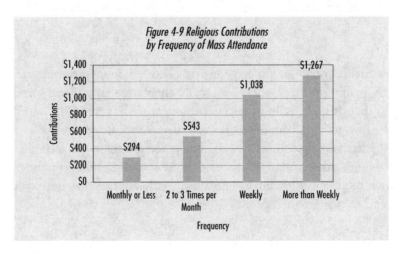

Figure 4-9 Religious Contributions by Frequency of Mass Attendance

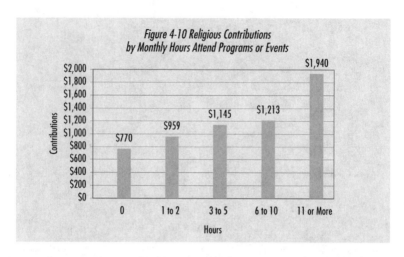

Figure 4-10 Religious Contributions
by Monthly Hours Attend Programs or Events

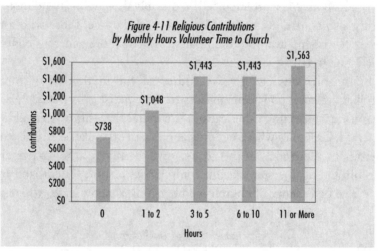

Figure 4-11 Religious Contributions
by Monthly Hours Volunteer Time to Church

fellow parishioners found it easy to write a check to support the Church but were unwilling to dig in and contribute their time and talent. We don't doubt that this occurs, but those parishioners are in a minority. As Figure 4-11 illustrates, parishioners who volunteer more time to work in their parish also contribute more dollars. The perceived trade-off between time and dollars doesn't exist. Whatever is motivating church members to express their commitment by contributing their time is also motivating them to contribute their money.

Conclusions

This chapter has considered the effects that religious beliefs and commitment have on religious contributions. We observed that although the acceptance of the Church's beliefs and teachings is an important factor in motivating religious contributions, no one is suggesting that the Church change its teachings merely to raise more money. Yet the way the message is presented and emphasized can be crucial. For example, the Catholic Church teaches that it is important to follow the teachings of Jesus; that it is our obligation to try to change unjust social structures; and that participating in the tradition and the sacraments of the Church are critical. But those parishioners who believe the emphasis should be placed on the latter two of these contribute more than those who emphasize the message of following Jesus. Yet, Jesus would certainly encourage us to change unjust social structures and to participate in the sacraments. Without downplaying the importance of Jesus or changing its fundamental message, the Church might be able to attract more contributions by modifying how it is presented.

One message that the Church need not concern itself with is its teachings on sexual ethics. Although our findings partially support Andrew Greeley in that those who disagree with the Church's position on issues like abortion, birth control, and the ordination of women give less, the relationship is very weak. Certainly we can find no support for asserting that alienation with the hierarchy on these issues is a primary explanation for low Catholic giving.

As expected, we found a strong relationship between contributions and various measures of church commitment, like Mass attendance and reading church-sponsored publications. This doesn't mean that they cause greater contributions, but rather that giving to the Church is just another form that religious commitment takes.

It's comforting to know that the more committed church members are also the more generous. But in *Money Matters* we found that the most committed Catholics lag behind the most committed Protestants in their generosity to their church. For example, among those members who attend worship services more than once a week, the average contribution for an Assemblies of God household was $3,510; for Southern Baptists it was $3,416; Presbyterians gave $3,226; and Lutherans $2,840. For Catholics, the figure was $1,267. A similar pattern held for the other commitment measures. In fact, the discrepancy in giving between the Catholics and Protestants in our sample in some cases actually *increased* with their commitment. For example, let us compare Catholics and Lutherans. Among those who only attend services once a month, the average Catholic household contributions were about 60% of those of Lutheran households. But among those who attend more than once a week, Catholic giving was only 45% of Lutheran giving. Priests who speak at Mass about the importance of religious commitment are frequently accused of "preaching to the converted." But while we need to continually affirm our most dedicated church members, we have to impress upon them that they can do better, at least with respect to their financial commitment.

References

D'Antonio, William, James Davidson, Dean Hoge, and Ruth A. Wallace. *American Catholic Laity in a Changing Church*. Kansas City: Sheed & Ward, 1989.

Greeley, Andrew M., William C. McCready, and Kathleen McCourt. *Catholic Schools in a Declining Church*. Kansas City: Sheed & Ward, 1976.

Hilke, John C. "Voluntary Contributions and Monitoring Efforts: Revealed Preference for the Services of Religious Organizations," *Journal for the Scientific Study of Religion*, Vol. 19, No. 2, 1980, pp. 138-45.

Hoge, Dean R., and Fenggang Yang. "Determinants of Religious Giving in American Denominations: Data From Two Nationwide Surveys," *Review of Religious Research*, Vol. 36, No. 2 (December, 1994), pp. 123-48.

Hoge, Dean R., Charles E. Zech, Patrick McNamara, and Michael J. Donahue. *Money Matters: Personal Giving in American Churches*. Louisville: Westminster/John Knox, 1996.

Iannaccone, Laurence R. "Why Strict Churches Are Strong," *American Journal of Sociology*, Vol. 99, No. 5 (March, 1994), pp. 1180-1211.

5

DENOMINATIONAL PROGRAMS AND PROCESSES

Of the many studies that have been conducted on Catholic religious giving, none have considered the effect of the larger Church's programs and decision-making processes (as opposed to their teachings) on parishioners' giving. We can only assume that this neglect is intentional. Maybe it has resulted from researchers' belief that Catholics uniformly love their Church and are unquestionably loyal to its leadership. Or it might be the opposite — maybe they believe that Catholics are frustrated with the hierarchical decision-making structure of the Church and have tuned it out of their own religious contributions decision-making process. Or maybe it reflects their opinion that the programs and processes of the larger Church are simply too distant and not relevant to the everyday lives of most Catholics. Eugene Kennedy (1995), for example, has asserted that an increasing number of Catholics are becoming what he has labeled "Culture Two Catholics." These are devoted Catholics who proclaim their faith through their everyday lives but are totally disinterested in the activities of the Church bureaucracy. Kennedy describes them as "individuals whose Catholicism is internalized."

Whatever the reason, it seems strange that researchers haven't even investigated the question of the role that the larger Church plays in explaining low Catholic contributions. This is especially unusual in light of the findings that the programs and processes of Protestant denominations have been shown to impact their members' giving patterns. For example, alienation with their denomination's programs and processes, as opposed to their teachings, has been shown to be an important factor in explaining the decrease in voluntary contributions that many Protestant congregations have been willing to make to support their denominationally sponsored programs, such as missions (Vallet and Zech, 1995).

For whatever reason, there is a gap in our understanding of the relationship between the programs and processes of the larger Church and members' contributions to their parish. This chapter addresses that gap by considering the effect of Catholic attitudes towards the larger Church's programs, and especially its decision-making processes, on their religious contributions. Throughout this discussion we will be comparing our Catholic samples' opinion on their church's programs and processes with those of our respondents from the four Protestant denominations in our study. It is important to keep in mind that ecclesiastically the Catholic Church is the most hierarchical church in this group.

Denominational Programs

As with most other religions, the vast majority of Catholic church programs are offered at the local, parish level. Preparation for the sacraments, prayer and study groups, ministries in music, evangelization, and church-sponsored social programs are all primarily parish-level activities. Dioceses support parish activities in these areas and others, such as parish administration. Dioceses also offer services that at various times impact on the lives of everyday Catholics. These include diocesan-sponsored schools (often high schools), hospitals, and social-service agencies such as nursing homes or homes for unwed mothers. Besides supporting diocesan efforts, the Church in Rome undertakes some activities directly, for example, the support of missionaries. Catholics are asked, through special monthly collections, to support Church-sponsored causes outside the parish, such as the American Bishops' Overseas Appeal, Peter's Pence (the pope's discretionary spending fund), and the retirement fund for religious sisters. But few Catholics have direct knowledge of these programs or how the money is spent.

In recent years the Church has become more vocal in taking stands on controversial social issues. Pope John Paul II has been a frequent newsmaker through his many travels and his willingness to speak to local concerns during these visits. He has shown a willingness to provide a clear and unequivocal message not only on matters of faith and morals, but also on peace and justice issues through his encyclicals and other public pronouncements. Since the early 1980s, the U.S. Catholic Bishops have been at the forefront of the debate on U.S. policy with their pastoral letters on peace (1983) and on economic justice (1985).

The point is that when Catholics are asked their opinion of the denominational-level activities of the Church, they are most likely thinking of diocesan-sponsored social-service programs, the support of foreign missions, or their view of the public pronouncements of the pope and bishops. They seldom have direct knowledge of the support functions played by the various denominational levels.

We asked our sample about how much enthusiasm they felt for the work and programs of the denomination. Nearly two-thirds (64%) gave the denominational programs either a very high or moderately high rating. This placed the Catholic Church's denominational approval rating slightly below that of the Assemblies of God (71%) and Southern Baptists (69%), but above that of Presbyterians (57%) and Lutherans (57%). This is noteworthy in that the Catholic Church is the most hierarchical of all the denominations in our sample. In fact, one of the distinguishing features of both the Assemblies of God and the Southern Baptists is their de-emphasis of any denominational hierarchy. When compared to Presbyterians and Lutherans, two churches where there is some connection between the local church and the denomination, Catholics are much more satisfied with their denomination's programs.

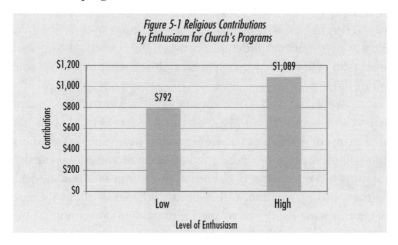

Figure 5-1 Religious Contributions by Enthusiasm for Church's Programs

As it turns out, satisfaction with the works and programs of the Catholic Church beyond the parish does influence giving. Figure 5-1 shows that Catholics who indicate enthusiasm for the larger Church's programs give more than those who don't. So Catholics aren't indifferent to the efforts of the Church beyond their parish, and whether or not they like the denomination's programs does play a role in their decision to contribute.

Denominational Decision-Making Processes

As we indicated in the opening chapter, some observers have blamed low Catholic giving on the laity's dissatisfaction with their level of participation in the Church's decision-making processes, both in general and in particular with respect to financial affairs. The decision-making issue can be considered from two perspectives: the denominational level and the parish level. Here, we consider satisfaction with denominational-level decision-making and its effect on contributions. In the next chapter, we assess the relationship between parish decision-making processes and giving.

We asked our lay sample a series of related questions concerning lay input into denominational decision-making. First, we asked about general decision-making processes. In our sample, fewer than half (49%) felt they had sufficient influence in the Church's decision-making process. This was well below the figure for the other four denominations that we studied. In each of them, about two-thirds of the laity felt they had sufficient influence. But any concern that the laity may feel with regard to their lack of influence was not evident in their decision to contribute to the Church. There was no significant difference between the household contributions of those who believed that they had enough influence and those who felt that they did not.

Next, we asked about the division of decision-making authority between the denomination and the parish. About one-third of our sample liked the current division of decision-making authority; 44% of our sample thought more decision-making should be made at the local parish level; and about 4% wanted more decision-making at the denominational level. The others had no opinion. This placed Catholics at about the midway point on this issue compared to the Protestants in our sample. A greater proportion of the Assemblies of God and Southern Baptists liked the current division in their denomination, while a smaller proportion of Presbyterians and Lutherans liked the current situation. All except the Assemblies of God would like more parish-level authority than the Catholics in our sample. Is this an important factor in influencing religious contributions? Yes. As Figure 5-2 indicates, those Catholics who are satisfied with the current division of decision-making authority contribute significantly more than those who prefer either more parish-level or more denominational-level authority.

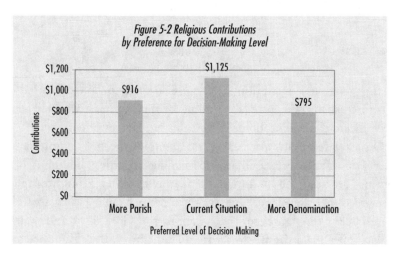

Figure 5-2 Religious Contributions by Preference for Decision-Making Level

What about decision-making specifically regarding church finances? Only about one-third of our Catholic sample thought they had enough information about the denomination's handling and allocation of funds. This is a very low figure. It compares with 46% for both the Lutherans and Presbyterians and slightly more than half of the Assemblies of God and Southern Baptists. But this is an important issue. Those who felt they did have enough information contributed significantly more than others (Figure 5-3).

We asked our sample if they trusted the denomination leaders' handling and allocation of funds. About 46% of the Catholics in the sample indicated a high level of trust. Another 45% demonstrated a medium level of trust. This was similar to the figure for the other denominations, except for the Assemblies of God, where more than two-thirds of the sample displayed a high degree of trust. But this turned out not to be an issue

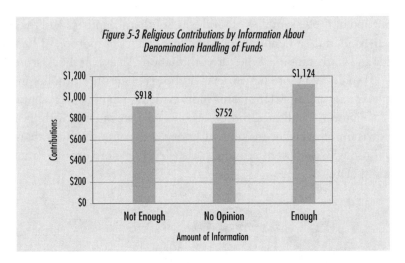

Figure 5-3 Religious Contributions by Information About Denomination Handling of Funds

affecting religious contributions. Because so many people exhibited high levels of trust in their leaders' handling of funds, giving was not significantly different for households with differing degrees of trust.

On a related matter, we asked our sample whether denominational leaders are sufficiently accountable to members regarding how church contributions are used. About 44% of the Catholics either strongly or moderately agreed that they were. This was the same percentage as Presbyterians, but well below the figures for the Assemblies of God (62%) and Southern Baptists (56%), and slightly lower than Lutherans (50%). But once again, it didn't seem to make much difference. Household contributions of those who gave the Church a high rating on accountability didn't differ significantly from those who gave it a low rating.

Finally, we asked two "bottom-line" questions about decision-making in the denomination. We asked if the leadership of the denomination was doing a good job. Almost three-fourths (71%) of our Catholic sample either strongly or moderately agreed that they were. This was below the approval rating for the Assemblies of God (82%), but well above that of the Presbyterians (54%), Lutherans (66%), and Southern Baptists (60%). Again, this is striking, given the very hierarchical nature of the Catholic Church. The leaders of the Church — most notably Pope John Paul II, but also including the local bishops — are evidently very popular and enjoy a great deal of support from the laity. Does this matter when it comes to giving to the Church? Yes. Figure 5-4 illustrates that those who agreed

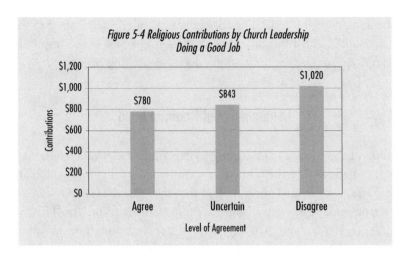

Figure 5-4 Religious Contributions by Church Leadership Doing a Good Job

that the denominational leadership was doing a good job contributed significantly more than those who either disagreed or weren't sure.

The other "bottom-line" question concerned the decision-making processes in the denomination. A much smaller proportion of Catholics (54%) approved of their denomination's decision-making process than approved of their denominational leadership. The leaders are more popular than the processes that they oversee. This placed Catholics about in the middle of the approval rating for denominational decision-making processes. They were tied with the Lutherans (also 54%), ahead of the Presbyterians (49%), but trailing both the Assemblies of God (70%) and the Southern Baptists (62%). Again, the question is, does it matter in

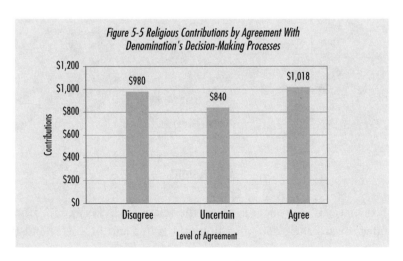

Figure 5-5 Religious Contributions by Agreement With Denomination's Decision-Making Processes

determining contributions? The answer is a qualified yes. Figure 5-5 shows that household contributions were slightly higher for those respondents who approved of the denomination's decision-making processes.

Denominational Financial Need

One of the theories attempting to explain low Catholic giving is that Catholics believe that the Church is wealthy and really doesn't need their contributions. We asked our sample if they thought the Church as a whole had serious financial needs. Slightly more than half said yes. This was a much larger percentage than any of the other denominations in our sample. About 44% of the Presbyterians, 42% of both the Lutherans and Southern Baptists, and 22% of the Assemblies of God felt that their denomination had serious financial needs. Does this affect Catholics' willingness to give? The answer is yes. Catholics who were convinced that the Church does have serious financial needs contributed significantly more than those who didn't believe it does or simply didn't know (Figure 5-6).

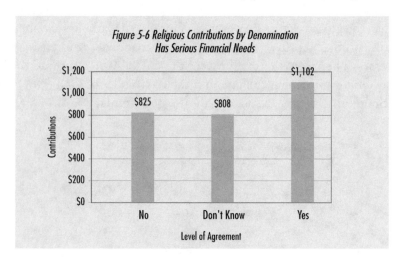

Figure 5-6 Religious Contributions by Denomination
Has Serious Financial Needs

Conclusions

So what can we conclude about the relationship between Catholics' attitudes toward their denomination's programs and processes and their willingness to contribute to their churches? Do Catholics approve of how their denomination is run, and if so, does it affect their giving?

The Catholics in our sample gave generally high ratings to denominational-level programs (at least to the extent they understood them). Those who liked the denomination's programs contributed more.

With regards to Church processes, though, the evidence is mixed and open to interpretation. On the one hand, Catholics (both on an absolute level and relative to the other denominations in our sample) felt they did not have sufficient influence in Church decision-making, lacked information on how Church funds were spent, and didn't think denominational leaders were accountable on how contributions were used. But for all three of these factors, there was either no significant impact on household contributions or those who were satisfied with the processes contributed more. One way to interpret this seeming contradiction is to conclude that Catholics really don't want any role in their Church's decision-making processes. Just because someone feels that they lack information on how funds are spent doesn't necessarily mean they think they should have that information. They might be just as happy not knowing. Perhaps they possess a strong belief in a hierarchical church and are willing to place unquestioning trust in their leadership.

The other interpretation is that many Catholics do want an input into the Church's decision-making processes. Their contributions are low because they feel shut out of some basic decisions, such as how their contributions are spent. According to this interpretation, if Church processes were more open, and the laity had more of a say, contributions would increase.

Both sides of this debate can find evidence in this chapter to support their interpretations. Those who support the current situation, with the laity receiving relatively little information and exerting little influence on Church decision-making, can point to the fact that the Catholic leadership received a very high rating, and a majority of the Catholics in our sample (54%) did approve of current denominational decision-making processes.

Those who believe Catholics should have more input into the Church's decision-making processes could point out that, in many instances, the Catholics in our sample gave their church the lowest approval on issues of openness of denominational decision-making processes, compared to the four Protestant denominations in the study. All four Protestant denominations receive significantly higher contributions from their members than does the Catholic Church. They could also point to the fact that more Catholics in our sample (44%) expressed a preference for more decision-making at the parish level, as opposed to 33% who preferred the current division of decision-making authority.

The tension between the laity and the hierarchy over the amount of influence the laity should have is one that cuts across many dimensions of Church life, not just finances. D'Antonio et al. (1996) asked their sample of Catholics whether the laity should have the right to participate in the decision-making for a broad range of issues. These included church finances, but also included selecting their parish priests and making policy about divorce, birth control, and women's ordination. For each of these, more than 60% of the respondents thought the laity should participate. We pick up on this issue in the next chapter when we examine the relationship between decision-making at the parish level and contributions.

References

D'Antonio, William V., James D. Davidson, Dean R. Hoge, and Ruth A. Wallace. *Laity: American and Catholic*. Kansas City: Sheed & Ward, 1996.

Kennedy, Eugene. *Tomorrow's Catholics, Yesterday's Church*. Liguori, MO: Triumph Books, 1995.

Vallet, Ronald E., and Charles E. Zech. *The Mainline Church's Funding Crisis: Issues and Possibilities*. Grand Rapids, MI: William B. Eerdmans, 1995.

6

PARISH PROGRAMS AND PROCESSES

The issues that have been covered so far in this book can be considered to some extent to be merely laying the groundwork. In many ways they can be likened to the preliminary fights at a boxing match. Some are more interesting than others, but most observers know that the real action will occur in the main event. When it comes to religious giving, the main event is at the parish level. Personal characteristics and beliefs, as we have seen, can play an important role. Most practicing Catholics cherish their denominational affiliation, and many are influenced by Church leadership, programs, and policies. But the parish is really where the Church has the greatest ability to impact individual religious giving.

This chapter considers a variety of parish-level characteristics that affect religious contributions. They are especially important because many of them (parish programs, the quality of preaching and liturgies, decision-making processes, stewardship programs, etc.) could realistically undergo adjustments without affecting any of the basic underlying truths of the Catholic faith. Also, the Church (depending somewhat on the individual diocese) grants pastors a relatively large degree of autonomy (some are referred to as "the popes of their parish"). From a policy perspective, the topics discussed in this chapter offer many more opportunities for innovation than do those discussed elsewhere in this book. Most of those other topics are, for ecclesiastical and practical reasons, beyond the scope of anyone interested in making changes in order to increase Catholic giving. It's at the parish level that the greatest strides can be made to induce Catholics to increase their giving.

Parish Size

The belief that the large size of Catholic parishes inhibits giving has become virtually a universal truth. Nearly every researcher who has considered the relationship between parish size and contributions has concluded that large Catholic parishes are associated with low Catholic giving. In fact, some have concluded that it is the single biggest reason to explain low Catholic giving relative to that of Protestants (see Zaleski and Zech, 1994; Hoge and Augustyn, 1997).

Three reasons are generally cited for this finding. The first is that large parishes suffer from congestion. This decreases the quality of parish-level activities. In large parishes parishioners may be unable to make an appointment to meet with a priest on a timely basis. The reception of some sacraments might be less personalized. For example, there might be three or four children receiving the Sacrament of Baptism at a particular service, rather than just one; two or three weddings scheduled for a particular Saturday; or (this might be wishful thinking in this day and age) long lines to receive the Sacrament of Reconciliation. Congestion might also occur at non-sacramental parish activities, reducing some members' enjoyment and willingness to participate. Congestion means that not all parishioners can fit into the church at the same Mass, requiring multiple Sunday Masses. This diminishes the parish's ability to foster a sense of community. And, of course, getting out of the parking lot after Sunday Mass can be a near occasion of sin for many Catholics.

A second reason is that large parishes impede the development of a sense of ownership among the parishioners. Parishioners need to feel that the parish is "theirs" in order to fully support it. They need to believe that they have a say in matters such as liturgy, parish programs, budgets, etc. Protestants contribute more, it is argued, because their smaller congregations give each member a greater sense of ownership, and therefore a greater sense of urgency, over what happens in the congregation. In many denominations, this even extends to the right to select their own pastor.

Finally, large parishes are believed to hamper giving because they lead to a behavior called "free-riding." This occurs when parish members, seeing the large membership in their church, say to themselves, "Look at all the people who belong to this parish and support it. Surely no one will notice, and the Church won't be affected, if I contribute less than I am able." Naturally, a few free-riders won't have much of an impact. But the larger the parish, the greater the tendency for many parishioners to become free-riders. This does not necessarily mean that they don't contribute at all (although parishes typically have a large number of households on their rolls who in fact don't contribute anything). Rather, free-ridership results in members contributing less than they could.

The myth that large parishes, because of congestion, the inability to develop a sense of ownership, and free-ridership, receive lower giving has been supported elsewhere. What did we find? We found that medium-sized parishes (1,001 to 2,500 members) receive significantly larger per-household contributions than do either smaller or larger parishes (Figure 6-1).

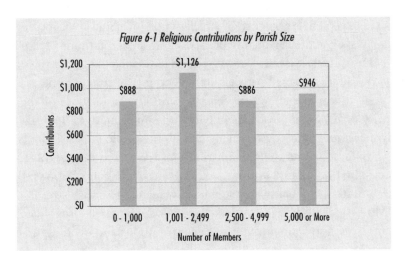

Figure 6-1 Religious Contributions by Parish Size

Members of the very largest parishes (more than 5,000 members) were the next most generous. Households belonging to the smallest parishes (1,000 or fewer members) were among the lowest givers. Incidentally, this same trend prevailed when we compared giving with parish size as measured by the number of households. Again, medium-sized parishes received greater per-household contributions than either larger or smaller parishes, but those differences were not statistically significant.

This pattern has been found elsewhere. Jeff Rexhausen and Michael Cieslak (1994) studied giving among parishes in the Cincinnati archdiocese. They found that household contributions were greater in medium-sized parishes (membership of 1,001 to 2,000 in their sample) than in either larger or smaller parishes. In fact, household contributions in the smallest parishes were the lowest.

The myth that large Catholic parishes are a cause of low Catholic giving can only be partially supported. We certainly can't support the myth that they are the primary cause. There is an optimal parish size somewhere in the range of 1,000 to 2,500 members. Parishioners in larger parishes contribute less, but so do members of smaller parishes. Not much has been written about low giving in smaller parishes, because other studies have generally concluded that small parishes are good. They offer less congestion, more of a sense of ownership, and less free-riding. We can only speculate as to why giving would be low in small parishes. It might be because small parishes lack the resources to offer a broad range of programs. Perhaps opportunities for parish involvement are blocked by small groups and cliques. Maybe they are routinely assigned lower-quality priests. There are a multitude of explanations. But it is clear that, at least with regard to their ability to cultivate monetary contributions, small parishes are no better than large parishes.

Why the discrepancy between these findings and those of the vast majority of other studies? One obvious reason is methodological. This study measured giving by surveying a random sample of parishioners and asking their actual household contributions. As stated earlier, this might have resulted in inflated estimates of per-household contributions. But it is doubtful that any bias was systematically related to parish size.

Most other studies, in contrast, have calculated per-household contributions by simply taking total parish contributions and dividing them by the total number of parish households. This can lead to inaccuracies. Parishes differ widely in their willingness and ability to keep accurate statistics on the number of registered households. Some parishes keep close tabs on households joining and leaving the parish. Other parishes seldom "clean their rolls," and may continue to list deceased members or those who have moved away long after the event. Actually, the case could be made that larger parishes have the most difficulty keeping track of the comings and goings of their parishioners. As a result, the number of households registered in Catholic parishes is virtually a random variable, related to how recently they have cleaned their rolls. Any calculation based on that figure is subject to error. In fact, the American Congregational Giving Study collected data on both total parish contributions and the number of registered parish households. When we calculated per-household giving by merely dividing contributions by registered households and compared it to parish size, we also got the result that the larger the parish, the lower the giving. However, we rejected this approach (and its resulting outcome) because we didn't believe the denominator (registered households), and therefore the value of per-household contributions, was reliable.

Parish Programs and Activities

Parish Programs

It is part of the conventional wisdom that parish programs and services positively affect contributions. Parishioners respond to good programs in general. They especially respond when their parish offers a particular program where they have an interest, where they can find a niche. But this hypothesis has received little empirical support. This may be because of the difficulty in collecting data on the quantity and quality of programs. Some researchers have considered the impact of paid parish staff on contributions, but their findings were ambiguous (see Zaleski and Zech, 1994, and Cieslak, 1984).

We asked our sample about parish programs. First, we asked the parishes about the extent to which they offered 12 different programs, including various types of children's and adult education, prayer groups, men's groups, women's groups, seniors' groups, singles' groups, etc. Only one, the sponsorship of prayer or study groups at church, significantly affected contributions (Figure 6-2). We also asked about the total number

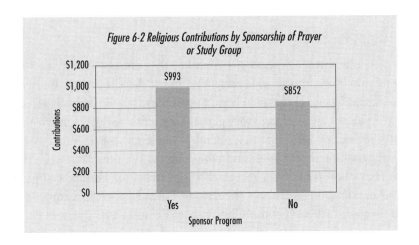

Figure 6-2 Religious Contributions by Sponsorship of Prayer or Study Group

of programs. We hypothesized that more programs would attract larger contributions, because they would increase the chances of someone finding a niche in the parish. But the number of programs was not significantly related to contributions.

We asked our sample about their general level of enthusiasm for their parish's programs. As Figure 6-3 demonstrates, people who were the most enthusiastic about the work of their parish contributed significantly more than those who lacked enthusiasm. So, even though we were unable to specify the number or type of programs that induce parishioners to contribute, we can confirm the conventional wisdom that parishioners who like their parish's programs do contribute more.

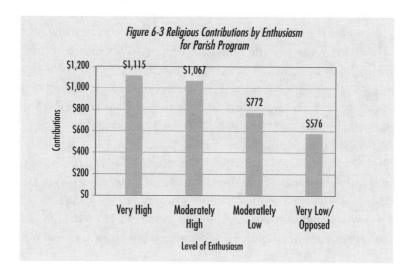

Figure 6-3 Religious Contributions by Enthusiasm for Parish Program

Liturgy

There are other aspects of parish life that are not exactly programs, but fall into the same general category. One of these is liturgy. It's been 40 years since Vatican II completely revamped the Catholic Mass. It's changed from a passive, nonparticipatory gathering performed in a foreign tongue to a more active, participatory assembly rendered in the vernacular. Still today, parishioners can be found who long for the pre-Vatican II Masses that they cherished. They resent the appearance of guitars and popular music at Mass, and yearn for the days of Latin Masses, Gregorian chant, and incense. Others feel the Church hasn't changed its liturgies enough.

They want an even more festive atmosphere, with a broader range of music and more lay participation. So, naturally, the question arises — are contributions affected by the traits of a parish's liturgies? The answer is no.

We asked our sample two related questions. One, aimed at those who yearn for "the good old days," asked if they'd contribute more if their parish's worship services were more traditional. Two-thirds said no. As Figure 6-4 shows, those who told us no gave significantly more. Does this mean that parishes should speed up their implementation of new, innovative liturgies? No. We also asked our sample if they would give more if their parish's worship services were more modern. Almost three-fourths (72%) indicated they wouldn't. Figure 6-5 reveals that those who said no to more modern liturgies also gave more.

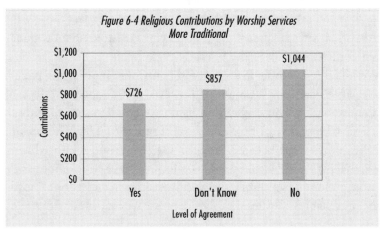

Figure 6-4 Religious Contributions by Worship Services More Traditional

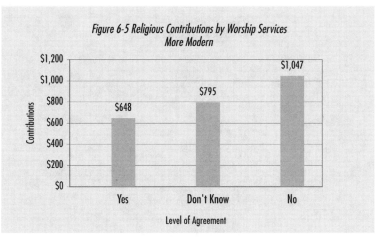

Figure 6-5 Religious Contributions by Worship Services More Modern

What can we conclude from the seemingly contradictory responses to this pair of questions? Catholics like their current liturgies. They don't want to go back to the old days of "bells and smells" Masses. Nor do they want different, trendy activities at their Masses. Parishes that can navigate a middle course between these two extremes will attract larger contributions.

Preaching

It is also widely accepted that religious contributions are related to the quality of the homilies that are preached each week. As with other goods and services, both secular and religious, quality is in the eyes of the beholder. For some, a quality homily is one that plays on some variation of a fire-and-brimstone theme. Others prefer homilies that speak to the struggles that they encounter as Christians trying to cope in a generally immoral or amoral society. In either case, one would expect those who are more satisfied with the preaching that they receive are also more generous when it comes to giving to the Church.

We asked our sample if they would contribute more if the preaching in their parish was more meaningful (however they defined it). Most (60%) said they wouldn't. Those who told us no contributed significantly more than those who said yes, or weren't sure (Figure 6-6). Does this mean that Catholics don't want better homilies? Or that, contrary to what most believe, the quality of homilies doesn't affect religious contributions? Probably not, although we didn't specifically ask either of those questions. Rather, it probably indicates that they're pretty well satisfied with the hom-

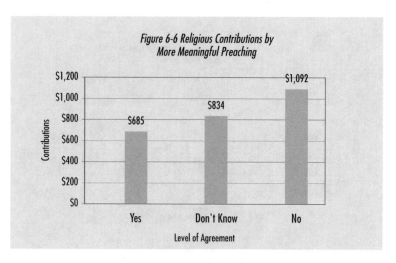

Figure 6-6 Religious Contributions by More Meaningful Preaching

ilies that they're currently receiving, and this is already reflected in their giving. Better homilies wouldn't have much of an additional impact on their decision to give.

Parish Message

Over time, a parish can develop the reputation for emphasizing a specific message. For example, some parishes become known for their outreach to the larger community. Others might be celebrated for their commitment to Catholic education. Still others might be renowned for their spirituality. In many cases, these had been the priority of long-term influential pastors. Parishioners came to identify with the messages those pastors brought and continued them even after the pastors had left.

We asked our sample about two possible themes. First, we asked whether they would contribute more if they found the parish to be more spiritually nourishing. More than half (54%) indicated no. Those who said no contributed significantly more than others (Figure 6-7).

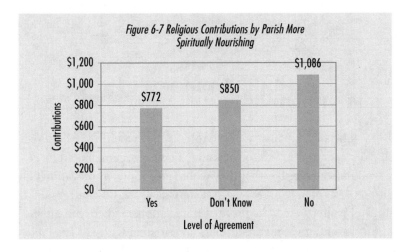

Figure 6-7 Religious Contributions by Parish More Spiritually Nourishing

Are we to conclude that parishioners don't want more spiritual nourishment? Of course not. We can probably interpret this response as similar to the response on preaching. Parishioners probably find their parishes to be spiritually nourishing, and have already factored that into their contributions.

The second theme we asked about was the parish's attention to social issues. We asked about the parish paying both more attention to social issues and less attention to social issues. This was to recognize that some Catholics are more otherworldly, while others think the Church should be more concerned with the social ills of this world.

The results were similar to the pair of questions that we asked about worship services. A majority of parishioners indicated that they would not give more if the parish paid more attention to social issues (57%). They contributed significantly more than those who said they would, or who didn't know (Figure 6-8).

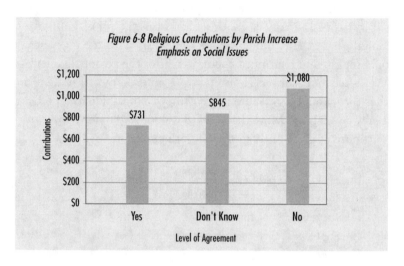

Figure 6-8 Religious Contributions by Parish Increase Emphasis on Social Issues

But a substantial majority (70%) told us they wouldn't give more if the parish paid less attention to social issues. They, too, contributed more than those who indicated either that they would give more, or they didn't know; the differences, though large, were not statistically significant. Again, these results can be interpreted like those of the relationship between satisfaction with liturgies and giving. Parishioners are satisfied with the level of social action in their parishes. They have already factored that satisfaction into their decision to contribute.

Parish Decision-Making Processes

Mirroring their hierarchical denominational structure, Catholic parishes have also had a history of top-down management. Whatever "Father said" became unquestioning parish policy, often simply because "Father said" it. It didn't seem to matter whether the issue concerned faith and morals, liturgies, parish spending, or even which political candidates to endorse.

Much of that has changed since Vatican II. Catholics now recognize that, through baptism, they not only have a right but an obligation to participate in parish decision-making. The Church is not a democracy, but the expectation is that parishioners will accept responsibility for the life of the parish through their participation on parish councils, finance committees, liturgy committees, and so on.

While much has changed in the realm of parish decision-making since Vatican II, not everything has. Some pastors still view themselves as the sole decision-maker in the parish and resent "lay intrusion." Many parishioners feel comfortable with the priest making all of their parish's decisions for them. Just because a parish claims on paper to have a parish council or a finance committee doesn't necessarily mean that shared decision-making is occurring.

In the previous chapter, we found that Catholics rate their input into denominational decision-making much lower than did the other denominations in our sample. But we also found that those who were satisfied with their role were more generous contributors. This combination could be used to support either of two radically different interpretations of the relationship between lay input into denominational decision-making processes and contributions. Are the same sort of relationships found at the parish level?

Parish Budgetary Processes

Our first interest is with preparing the parish budget. This is perhaps the most critical area for lay input. Budgetary decisions on how parish funds are spent set the tone for the parish and determine its priorities. Will the school get more money? What about the CCD program? Should we increase our support for CYO activities? How much should we allocate for outreach efforts to the less-fortunate members of our community? In parish life, as in government, "He who controls the purse strings controls the kingdom."

There are two separate but related aspects here: preparing the budget, and approving the budget. It's difficult to say which is more important. Though final approval implies the ability to make last-minute changes, in many cases these changes are marginal. And while those preparing the budget have the ability to set the agenda for the entire parish, their power is limited if their spending allocations can be overturned at the time of final approval.

We asked our sample of parishes about who had input into the preparation of the budget, and who had the final approval of the budget. The pastor was involved in the preparation of the budget in almost all of the parishes in our sample (94%). The parish-finance committee typically also had some input (83%). The paid staff participated in the preparation of the budget in only about half (52%) of the parishes. In only about a third of the parishes (34%) was the parish council involved. The rest of the parishioners assisted in the preparation of the budget in fewer than 10% of the parishes.

Who had the final approval? The pastor alone had the final approval of the budget in more than two-thirds (69%) of the parishes. In another 2% of the parishes the pastor shared final authority with the finance committee, and in 6% of the parishes the pastor, finance committee, and parish council jointly exercised final budgetary approval. The finance committee alone had the final say in 11% of the parishes. The parish council had that responsibility in 8% of the parishes. None of the parishes in our sample gave final approval to the parishioners as a group.

Does any of this make a difference in parishioners' contributions? Only in two cases. Parishes where the finance committee had input into developing the budget received significantly higher contributions than those where that committee was not involved (Figure 6-9). It didn't matter one way or another whether the pastor, parish council, staff, or general parish were part of the process.

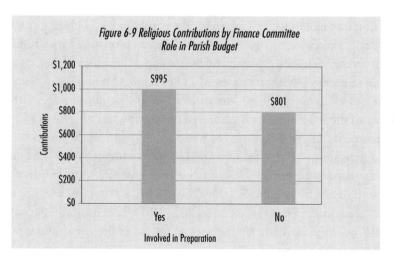

Figure 6-9 Religious Contributions by Finance Committee Role in Parish Budget

Second, parishes where the pastor was not involved in the final approval of the budget received higher per-household contributions than in those parishes where he assumed some responsibility, either by himself or in conjunction with other parish organizations (Figure 6-10).

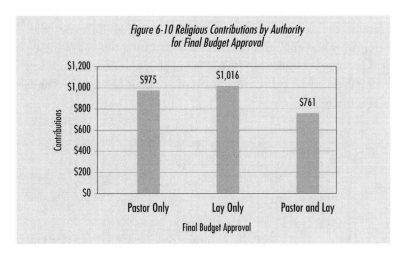

Figure 6-10 Religious Contributions by Authority
for Final Budget Approval

Attacking the issue from another perspective, we asked parishioners which they preferred, priests or laity handling parish financial matters. More than three-fourths (78%) responded that they favored a combination of priests and lay members. Those who supported a combination gave slightly less than those who preferred lay only. Both groups contributed significantly more than those who thought that priests alone should control parish finances (Figure 6-11).

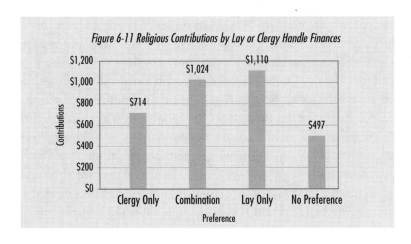

Figure 6-11 Religious Contributions by Lay or Clergy Handle Finances

Do parishioners think that they have enough information about the handling of funds in their parish? Since they are not a part of the budgetary process in most parishes, it's not surprising that only slightly more than half (53%) thought they did. This is well below the figure for the Protestants in our sample. In every other denomination in our sample, at least 70% (and in the case of Southern Baptists, more than 80%) of the respondents felt they had enough information concerning the handling of parish funds. Giving was significantly higher in those parishes where the laity believe that they had sufficient information about how parish funds were spent (Figure 6-12).

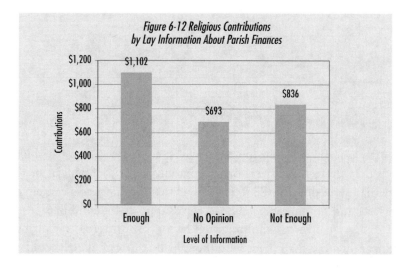

Figure 6-12 Religious Contributions by Lay Information About Parish Finances

But maybe Catholics are satisfied with their lack of information concerning parish financial matters. Maybe they're happy to have the parish budget dictated to them. Perhaps they don't want any input into parish financial decision-making. We asked our sample whether they thought parishioners had enough influence in parish financial decision-making. Fewer than half (48%) thought that they did. Again, this was considerably below the figure for the Protestants in our sample. More than two-thirds of the members of each of the other denominations (and more than three-fourths of the Southern Baptists) agreed that typical members had adequate influence in congregational financial issues. Possessing this influence made a difference in Catholic giving. Figure 6-13 shows us that those Catholics who believed that they had ample influence contributed more.

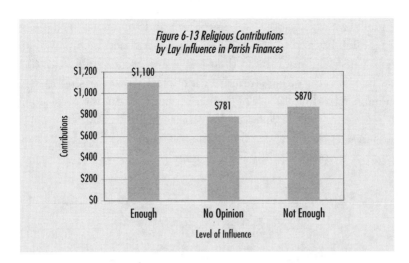

Figure 6-13 Religious Contributions
by Lay Influence in Parish Finances

It appears that Catholics, at least relative to Protestants, wish that laypeople had more say in parish financial matters. But given that they lack that input, are they satisfied with the parish budget that does emerge? We asked them if they thought their parish's budget priorities were acceptable. Barely more than half (53%) either strongly or moderately agreed that their parish's budget priorities were appropriate. This lagged behind the approval figures for the other denominations, which ranged from 69% (Lutherans) to 80% (Southern Baptists). And, once again, we find this to be a significant factor in determining Catholic contributions (Figure 6-14).

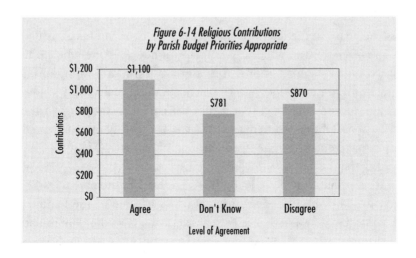

Figure 6-14 Religious Contributions
by Parish Budget Priorities Appropriate

Finally, we asked about two important and somewhat related issues: the accountability and trustworthiness of the parish leadership in financial matters. Most Catholics found their leadership accountable, with 61% of our sample agreeing either strongly or moderately that parish leaders were accountable regarding the use of their contributions. But the corresponding figure was more than 70% for each of the four Protestant denominations in the sample. Catholics who found their parish leadership to be accountable contributed significantly more (Figure 6-15).

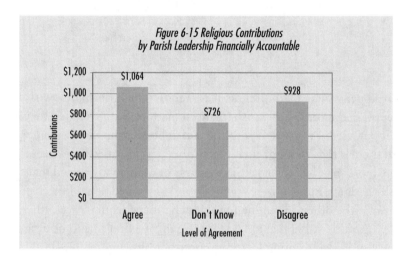

Figure 6-15 Religious Contributions by Parish Leadership Financially Accountable

It should go without saying that trustworthiness is a critical element across the board in the relationship between a pastor and his parishioners. This is especially true when it comes to money. Anyone who hopes to induce voluntary contributions from a group must, at a minimum, have the trust of that group. Parishioners have a natural inclination to want to trust their pastor. Most feel that if they can't trust their pastor with their contributions, whom can they trust? The vast majority of priests are holy and spiritual men and eminently deserving of that trust. Therefore, it's not surprising that nearly two-thirds of the Catholic parishioners in our sample indicated that they placed a high level of trust in the parish leadership (which would primarily be the pastor) when it came to the handling of their funds. Unfortunately, this is the lowest of any of the denominations in our sample. More than 80% of the Assemblies of God and Southern Baptists placed a high degree of trust in their congregational leadership. Is this because Catholic pastors are less worthy of this trust? No. The answer probably lies in the failure of Catholic pastors to provide information and accountability on parish financial matters. Throughout this section, we've seen that Catholics believe they have less information and that their leadership is less accountable to them than in Protestant congregations. All of this combined has resulted in lower levels of trust in their parish leadership. Does this affect contributions? Figure 6-16 shows that Catholics who had a high degree of trust in their leadership's ability to handle parish finances contributed more.

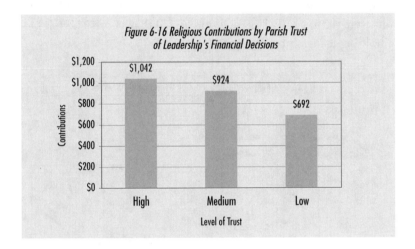

Figure 6-16 Religious Contributions by Parish Trust of Leadership's Financial Decisions

We asked the question in a myriad of ways, and each time we received the same answer: Catholic parishioners want more lay input into the financial decision-making process in their parish. They want the laity involved in both constructing and approving the budget. They want budget information disseminated. They want their pastors to be accountable to them as to how their parish spends its money. Parishioners who believe the budget process is open, who believe the typical layperson has some meaningful input into the parish financial decision-making process, will contribute more.

Other Parish Decision-Making

The Catholics in our sample sent us a clear message concerning their desire to be involved in their parish's decision-making process when money is involved. What about other parish activities? Do parishioners want the same level of input in other parish matters such as liturgy, evangelization, religious education, and so on? Generally speaking, the answer is yes. For example, we asked our sample if opportunities to serve in parish leadership roles were generally available. Some parishes are notorious for the fact that the pastor alone controls appointment to the key parish committees and their chairs. In other parishes, a small clique of laypeople might exert undue influence over parish committee appointments. Slightly more than 85% of the Catholics in our sample agreed that parish leadership opportunities were generally available. Although lower than the corresponding value for the Protestant denominations, it is still a very healthy level. Their contributions were significantly larger (Figure 6-17) than those who felt blocked from holding leadership positions.

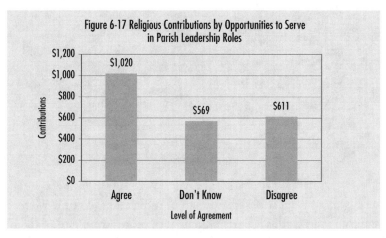

Figure 6-17 Religious Contributions by Opportunities to Serve in Parish Leadership Roles

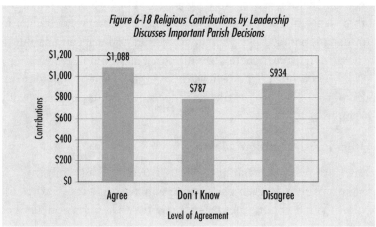

Figure 6-18 Religious Contributions by Leadership Discusses Important Parish Decisions

We also asked about the extent to which important parish decisions are made after an open discussion between the parish leadership and the members. Only 47% of our Catholic sample either strongly or moderately agreed that these discussions took place in their parish. In each of the Protestant denominations, nearly three-fourths of the respondents agreed that these discussions occurred. Figure 6-18 demonstrates that Catholics in those parishes where open discussions took place contributed at significantly higher levels.

Finally, we asked our sample if they approved of the overall decision-making process in their parish. While 72% expressed their approval, more than 80% of each of the Protestant denominations in our sample approved of their congregation's overall decision-making process. Catholics who approved of their parish's overall decision-making process contributed more, but the differences were not statistically significant.

From this we can conclude that lay Catholics respond favorably when they are given an input into overall parish decision-making, not just in the financial area. This positive reaction translates into larger contributions.

Parish School

Whether or not parish schools foster larger contributions from the parishioners is open to debate. We had some parishioners tell us about how critical the parochial school was to the life of the parish, how the school produces commitment to the parish, and how all parish activities centered around the life of the school. Other parishioners described their parochial school as a large vacuum cleaner that sucked up parish resources. They claimed that a large portion of the parish budget went toward the support of a program (the school) that served a small minority of the parishioners. This debate can become especially animated in suburban parishes, where many parishioners are paying high taxes to support their public school system and resent their religious contributions being used to support an (in their opinion) inferior educational alternative. This is also a controversial issue in some inner-city parishes, where a large percentage of the parochial school students are not Catholic, but are enrolled in the parish school to avoid substandard public schools.

A total of 69% of the parishes in our sample supported a parochial school, either by themselves (39%) or in conjunction with other parishes in a consolidated school (30%). The average annual cost incurred by those parishes that supported a school by themselves was $406,500. Most of this cost was covered by tuition revenue. The average was $225,900 (56% of total costs). Direct parish subsidies covered another $138,700 (34%). The remainder came from fundraising (7%) and other sources, including indirect subsidies (for example, sharing utility costs and janitorial services with the rest of the parish). Naturally, the costs for those parishes that cosponsored a consolidated parochial school were much lower — about $98,000 per parish in direct and indirect subsidies. The school subsidy in those parishes that had their own parochial school averaged about 27% of the parish budget. In those parishes with consolidated schools, the average subsidy was 20% of the parish budget.

What have other studies learned about the effect of parochial schools on parishioners' giving? Surprisingly little. In fact, most researchers didn't even examine the relationship between the existence of a school and contributions. Michael Welch (1993) is one who did. He expected that the existence of a school would positively impact both his measures of parishioners' religious participation (monetary contributions and parish activity involvement) and devotion (worship attendance and participation in religious rituals). But it had no meaningful affect on any of them except for a modest impact on their giving.

Jeff Rexhausen and Michael Cieslak (1994) also considered the effect of schools on giving. Using data from the Cincinnati archdiocese, they found that diocese-wide, there was a slight relationship between giving and the existence of a school in the parish. But they received some stronger results when they broke their sample down geographically. The existence of a school had no effect on giving in large city or suburban parishes. But it had a strong and positive effect on giving in small city and rural parishes. In fact, the existence of a school was the single most important determinant of giving in small-city parishes.

Dean Hoge and Boguslaw Augustyn (1997) considered the effect of parish schools on giving in their nationwide sample of 1,682 parishes. They found that the existence of a school in a parish was associated with higher per-household giving (p. 56). The existence of a school had its greatest impact on giving in small (500 or fewer households) and medium-sized (501 to 1,500 households) parishes, but a smaller effect on giving in large (over 1,500 households) parishes.

The other prominent researcher to investigate the relationship between parochial schools and giving was Greeley (1987). Remember, Bishop McManus had hypothesized that low Catholic giving could be attributed to the fact that Catholics were burdened by paying high parochial-school tuition. This, the bishop thought, was in lieu of larger contributions to their parish. Greeley's data contradicted that viewpoint. He found that households with children in Catholic schools contributed more (even after having paid tuition) than those without children in parochial schools. He even argued that their extra contributions were more than enough to pay the parish's subsidy, and that "Catholic schools not only supported themselves from higher Sunday contributions but indeed were a profitable enterprise for the Church" (p. 47).

There are really two related issues here. One concerns the contributions of those families who send their children to parochial schools. Do they contribute more, even after having made their tuition payments, than do other households? The other issue concerns the reaction of the entire parish to the school. Are parochial schools considered to be so essential in creating a sense of excitement and dynamism in a parish, are they so instrumental in enhancing not only the social life but also the spiritual life of the parish, that their very existence results in larger parishioner contributions? Or are they a massive drain on the parish's resources that causes resentment and thus lower contributions among the other parishioners?

We should emphasize that when we asked parishioners about the amount that they gave, we specifically asked that they not include any tuition payments. On the other hand, we know of some parishes in which the school tuition is kept artificially low, but parents are required to meet a certain standard in their regular giving. This is done to give parents a tax break. School tuition is not tax-deductible, but religious contributions are. This practice inflates the amount of contributions made by households with parochial school children. It is illegal, but it is done. We have no way of knowing the extent to which, if any, this tactic may have affected our results.

Figure 6-19 shows the answer to the first question. Households that send their children to parochial schools do contribute significantly more than do other households. The data doesn't allow us to say with any certainty that this difference in annual contributions (about $600 per household) is sufficient to cover the parish subsidy. So this result alone doesn't

allow us to support Greeley's claim that parochial schools are a profit center for parishes. But they certainly are consistent with his findings.

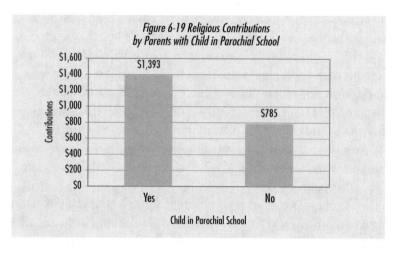

Figure 6-19 Religious Contributions by Parents with Child in Parochial School

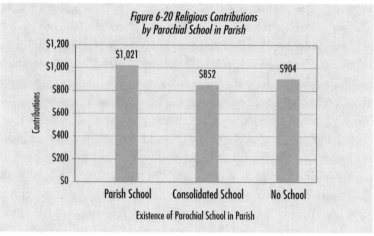

Figure 6-20 Religious Contributions by Parochial School in Parish

Is there support for Catholic schools as a boon to parish contributions,
rather than a source of resentment, when we look at the larger picture? Do
parishes that sponsor parochial schools receive larger contributions? A
qualified yes. As Figure 6-20 illustrates, parishes that operated their own
parochial school received significantly greater contributions per household
than did other parishes. Surprisingly, parishes that didn't offer a school
received higher contributions than parishes that cosponsored a consoli-

dated parochial school with other parishes. As an aside, we wondered whether the effect of the parochial school on giving was related to how much parishioners were being asked to subsidize the school. So we looked at the relationship between the subsidy burden, as measured by the percent of total parish revenue that was used to subsidize the parish school, and household contributions. There was no significant relationship. Parishioners' contributions are not related to the amount of burden that the parish might feel in supporting the school.

What can we make of this pattern? One conclusion is that parents who send their children to parochial schools are among the most committed in the parish, at least as measured by their giving. Whether this commitment to the parish is a consequence of the impact of the school on their social or spiritual lives, we can't be certain. In fact it could well be that the causality runs the other way. Maybe it's the case that those Catholics who are the most committed to the Church in the first place tend to send their children to parochial schools. Whatever the cause, Catholics who send their children to parochial schools are more generous in their contributions.

Not only that, but commitment and generosity spill over to the rest of the parish. The higher per-household contributions of parishes that sponsor their own school provides at least tacit support for the theory that many parishioners consider the parish school to be a source of enrichment for the parish at large. But this support doesn't extend to consolidated schools. Not only do parishes that cosponsor a school receive lower contributions than parishes with their own schools; they receive less than parishes without any school at all. Clearly, the value to the parish of a parochial school is not restricted to just the education it provides. Its impact on the everyday lives of the parish is also profound. But when the parishioners are not in direct (perhaps physical) contact with the school, these benefits are lost. Without the witness that the school provides, parishioners may come to resent the fact that their contributions are being used to support this "distant" project, just as they might resent their religious contributions being used to pay for a private academy. The consolidated school could be considered distant even if it happens to be physically located on parish grounds. The fact that it is shared with other parishes means that parishioners have lost their sense of involvement and ownership in the school. Just as "it takes a village to raise a child," it takes a parish. When that responsibility is shared with households from other parishes, some of the commitment is lost. That seems to be the task that parishes that cosponsor a consolidated school face. How to reconcile the fact that parish schools are expensive, and require a large amount of resources which the parish may not be able to afford on their own, with the need for the parish as a whole to feel a sense of involvement, even a sense of ownership, with the school? This is not an insurmountable task, but its critical nature must be recognized.

The fact that parishes with consolidated schools receive such low contributions shouldn't diminish the finding that parishes with their own parochial schools receive substantially larger contributions, both from families with children in the school and from other parishioners. In fact, it reinforces that finding. Greeley was right. Parochial schools seemingly do pay for themselves. Parishes considering merging their parochial school with nearby parishes should pay close attention to this fact.

Stewardship

Stewardship — the giving of our time, talent, and treasure to our church in recognition that all we have is really a gift from God — is one of the trendiest topics in Catholic parishes today. The Bible contains numerous allusions to positive rewards for good stewardship. Protestants have been emphasizing it for years, our parishioners are being told. It's time we Catholics caught up.

Unfortunately, to many pastors, "stewardship" and "money" are synonymous. Too often, stewardship is viewed as simply another fundraising technique. How often have you heard pastors say something like, "I know that contributions of time and talent are probably important too, but right now our real need in this parish is financial. So let's emphasize the money aspects of stewardship for now. We'll get to the time and talent part as soon as we're financially stable." Not only is this bad theology, it's bad fundraising. Appealing to the biblical precept of stewardship just to place another twist on a fundraising campaign runs the risk of alienating parishioners.

In Chapter 1, we noted that the U.S. bishops had received a considerable amount of criticism over their refusal to include some practical recommendations in their 1992 pastoral on stewardship. Perhaps anticipating that criticism, the bishops had included a disclaimer in the introduction:

"Concentrating on one specific obligation of stewardship, even one as important as church support, could make it harder — even impossible — for people to grasp the vision. It could imply that when Bishops get serious about stewardship, what they really mean is simply giving money" (NCCB, 1992, p. 5).

This is a legitimate concern. There are a number of formalized "Stewardship Programs" available for parishes to adopt. Most place their primary focus on the money portion of stewardship, giving only lip service to the time and talent components. For example, one of the most popular is "Sacrificial Giving." It consists of five elements:

1. Giving is Planned. It is part of a household's total financial plan that includes an intentional response to God's generosity.
2. Giving is Proportionate. While the tithe is the biblical standard, parishioners not prepared to be tithers are nevertheless encouraged to think in terms of contributing a percentage of their income.
3. Giving is Sacrificial. It should come from a household's substance, rather than its abundance.
4. Giving is Free. The giver places no conditions on the gift.
5. Giving is a Prayer of Thanksgiving. It is most appropriately presented at the Offertory of the Mass (Harris, 1994, p. 230).

You don't have to read too carefully to observe that there is no mention of time and talent. We've seen sacrificial-giving literature that does mention time and talent, but it is always done as an afterthought.

We don't mean to imply that all stewardship programs only emphasize the money component, or that all pastors view stewardship as a fundraising gimmick. We're only pointing out that the potential exists.

Besides focusing primarily on the financial impact of stewardship, there are other potential pitfalls that parishes considering introducing a stewardship program must avoid. Some of these revolve around the way the stewardship message is framed.

Stewardship is not about something we do; it's about who we are, and whose we are. Through our faith in Jesus Christ, we are children of God and joint heirs with Christ (see Romans 8:17). Nor is stewardship about merely meeting the parish budget; it's about examining our attitude toward and our use of money. Stewardship is not just about good intentions and kind deeds; it's about recognizing that all life depends on God. Finally, it's not just an annual campaign designed to induce people to contribute to the Church as yet another charity; it's about transformed visions, changed attitudes, and altered lives.

So how prevalent is stewardship in our sample of Catholic parishes? Sixteen percent of the parishes claimed to emphasize stewardship year-round. Another 44% emphasized it occasionally. This compares to the nearly 90% of the Protestant congregations in our sample who claimed to emphasize stewardship occasionally or year-round. Does emphasizing stewardship make a difference? Yes.

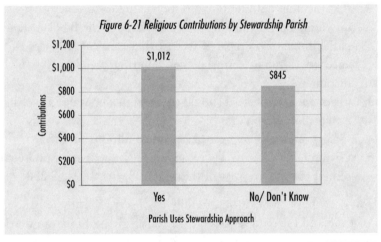

Figure 6-21 Religious Contributions by Stewardship Parish

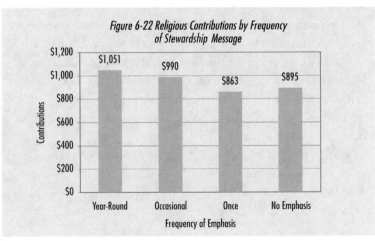

Figure 6-22 Religious Contributions by Frequency of Stewardship Message

We asked our sample whether their parish promoted stewardship and whether or not it affected their giving. As Figure 6-21 illustrates, parishioners who belonged to stewardship parishes contributed significantly more than those who didn't or weren't sure. How often does the stewardship message need to be heard? Figure 6-22 shows us that household contributions increased with more regular stewardship emphasis.

Pledging

What about the various tactics associated with successful stewardship programs? For example, how about the practice of filling out annual pledge cards? We heard a lot of resistance from parishioners when this topic was raised in our focus-group interviews. Those who opposed it didn't like the idea of giving as an obligation. Some told us that if their parish relied on pledging, it would actually receive less money. People's pledges would be lower than they're currently giving. They'd be afraid to pledge as much as they currently give because some unknown might occur that might prevent them from meeting their pledge. They were unconvinced when we tried to point out the inconsistency in their argument. Some of the same people who were violently opposed to an annual pledge to support their church wouldn't hesitate to commit themselves to a four-year car loan. Others reacted negatively to the thought of pledging to support current church operations, but gladly made two-or-three year pledges to fund a capital campaign.

We should note that many Protestants were also opposed to pledging and gave us the same reasoning as our Catholic focus groups. In fact, while 48% of the Catholics approved of the use of pledge cards, only 37% of the Assemblies of God and only 41% of the Southern Baptists did. Of course, these denominations teach that it is a Christian's duty to tithe. Pledging received a high approval rating among the Presbyterian sample (78%), but only moderate approval (58%) among Lutherans.

Does pledging among Catholics make a difference? Yes. Figure 6-23 shows that Catholics who approved of the practice of pledging contributed significantly more than others. In Figure 6-24, we see that those who actually filled out a pledge card gave at significantly higher levels.

A related issue concerns the extent to which Catholics plan their giving. Possibilities range from those Catholics who tithe to those who decide on Sunday morning how much they can afford to throw into the offertory

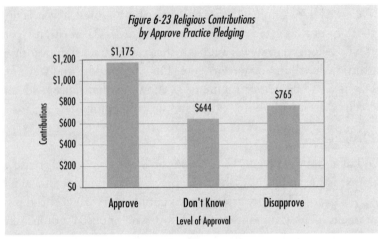

Figure 6-23 Religious Contributions by Approve Practice Pledging

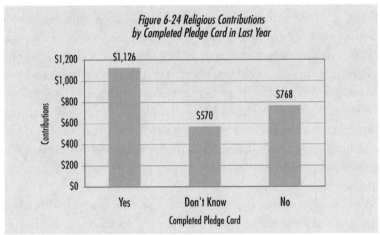

Figure 6-24 Religious Contributions by Completed Pledge Card in Last Year

basket that week. We'd expect that the more planning that goes into the religious-giving decision, the greater the level of contributions. This would be true even for those who aren't officially pledging. Figure 6-25 confirms this suspicion.

Those who tithed, of course, contributed the most. But those who had planned their giving for the year, either as a percentage of income or as an annual dollar amount, contributed more than those whose giving is based on a weekly decision. The more effective that parishes are in convincing their people to determine their giving on an annual basis, whether through formal pledges or informal commitments, the larger will be their contributions.

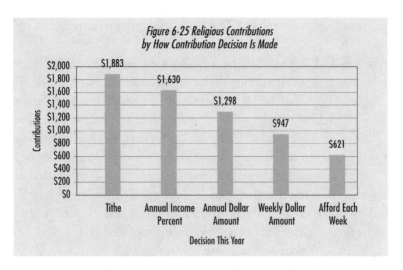

Figure 6-25 Religious Contributions
by How Contribution Decision Is Made

Other Stewardship Tactics

There are other practices that parishes could employ as part of their stewardship campaign. For example, priests could preach sermons on the topic of stewardship. Laypeople might be invited to give testimonials at Mass about what their stewardship commitment has meant in their lives. The parish could disseminate promotional materials, such as brochures. These could be either distributed at Mass or mailed to every parish household. The stewardship committee could make an effort to telephone or even personally visit parishioners to talk about stewardship with them. We asked our sample about each of these practices. None of them was significantly related to giving.

It is clear, then, that lay Catholics are responsive to the stewardship message. Adopting a stewardship approach is not only sound theologically, but it will also make a parish better off financially. Though there is some resistance to the concept of pledging (or filling out "commitment cards") among lay Catholics, parishioners who do pledge contribute more. But other stewardship techniques were unsuccessful in raising the level of contributions.

Parish Financial Need

Perhaps the antithesis of stewardship is an appeal for funds based on parish needs. This is a frequent tactic used by fundraisers. They try to convince the donor that their cause is in serious financial straits. They appeal to the donor's sense of responsibility to make sure that this worthwhile endeavor is financially solvent. Donors respond out of a feeling of obligation or guilt.

We saw in Chapter 4 that Catholics were more concerned than the others in our sample about their denomination's financial condition. Those who thought the Church had serious financial needs contributed more. At the parish level, just under 40% of our sample of Catholic parishioners thought that their parish had either serious or very serious financial needs. This was similar to the figure in our other four denominations. Is the message of parish financial need effective in increasing contributions? Yes. Parishioners who felt that their parish had some financial need contributed more than others (Figure 6-26). Appealing to the parishioners on the basis of parish financial need is not a stewardship message. But it can be effective if the parish's goal is to increase contributions.

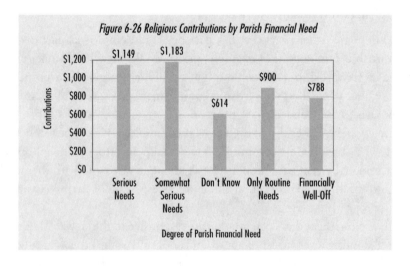

Figure 6-26 Religious Contributions by Parish Financial Need

Parish Teachings

Another one of the possible determinants of religious giving that has received little or no attention is the effect of individual parish teachings.

The Catholic Faith discourages variance from official Church dogma; no one would suggest that a parish should compromise Church doctrine merely to increase giving. But individual parishes have been known to place different emphases on some Church precepts. For example, in Chapter 4, we saw that when we asked our sample what the primary duty of Christians was, different responses were associated with different contribution levels. Of the four options that were provided, those who believed that their primary duty was to participate in Church traditions and sacraments were the highest givers. They were followed closely by those who believed that their primary duty was to change unjust social structures. To understand that issue from another angle, we asked the pastors in our sample which of the four possible messages did they emphasize in their parish. A large majority, 62%, said that of the alternatives provided, their primary emphasis was on following the teachings of Jesus as a basis for spiritual growth and fulfillment. Another 30% emphasized faithfully participating in the tradition and sacraments of the Church. This was no surprise; the Catholic Church is very sacramental, and its teachings have historically relied on tradition. Only 5% indicated that their parish primarily emphasized helping others commit their lives to Christ, which is the response that we would have expected from some of the more conservative, evangelical Christians. Just 3% chose the more liberal response by indicating that their parish was primarily concerned with helping to change unjust or oppressive social structures. All are legitimate emphases and all are consistent with Catholic Church teachings. But the different nuances could affect giving. In fact, they do, as Figure 6-27 reveals. While changing unjust social structures was the least likely response, members of parishes that emphasized that message contributed the most.

We also asked our pastors about their ecumenical teachings. Eighty-three percent indicated that they thought the Catholic Church was the one true church, and only 16% believed that other Christian faiths are

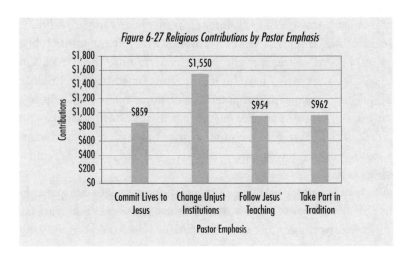

Figure 6-27 Religious Contributions by Pastor Emphasis

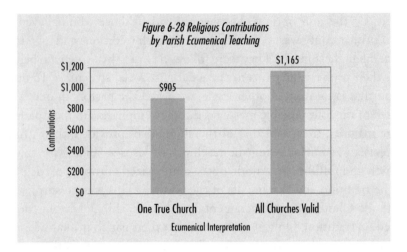

Figure 6-28 Religious Contributions by Parish Ecumenical Teaching

equally valid. But, as shown in Figure 6-28, members of those parishes with the more ecumenical attitude contributed more.

Finally, we asked the pastors to compare their parish's teachings with those of a "typical" Catholic parish. Eighty percent said they were similar; 13% indicated that they allow more differences in interpreting Church teachings than other Catholic parishes; and 7% declared that they were probably stricter in interpreting Church teachings. Members of those parishes that allowed more flexibility in interpreting Church teachings tended to contribute more than the others, although the differences were not statistically significant.

The Pastor

Pastors can make a huge difference in the quality of parish life. There are legions of examples of cradle Catholics who left the Church because they disapproved of the way the pastor was running the parish. On the other hand, some pastors have built enormous reputations for their seeming ability to pull a parish through difficult times single-handedly. A poor pastor can do a lot of damage, but an excellent pastor can make up for a multitude of deficiencies in the other aspects of parish life. This fact is perhaps so obvious that few researchers have considered the pastor's impact on parish giving.

Michael Welch (1993), for example, did not directly ask parishioners about their opinions of their pastor. Rather, he asked about satisfaction with the quality of pastoral care in the parish. This would certainly include the contribution of the pastor, but would also include parishioners' ratings of associate pastors and lay staff. He found that there wasn't a significant relationship between this variable and parish giving.

An interesting twist on the role that pastors play can be found in a study done by Michael Cieslak (1994). He considered the effect on giving when a parish experienced a change in its pastor. The loss of a popular pastor might decrease contributions, whereas replacing an unpopular pastor might increase parish income.

Cieslak studied the 106 parishes of the Rockford, Illinois, diocese during the period 1980 to 1993. He found that parishes did achieve a significant change in giving (either up or down) when a new pastor was appointed. The largest change tended to occur during a pastor's first year at his parish. The change in giving associated with the appointment of a new pastor was greatest in rural and suburban parishes, those with wealthier parishioners, parishes with younger members, those that did not have an elementary school (either on their own or a consolidated school), and those whose previous pastor had served at least 12 years. These results support the contention that a pastor can have an impact on parish giving.

What were our findings? For one thing, Catholic parishioners generally liked their pastor. About 87% either strongly or moderately agreed that their pastor had done a good job. This was in line with the other denominations in our sample. Did this matter? As Figure 6-29 illustrates, yes, it did. Parishioners who were more satisfied with their pastor contributed significantly more. Satisfaction with the pastors did make a difference!

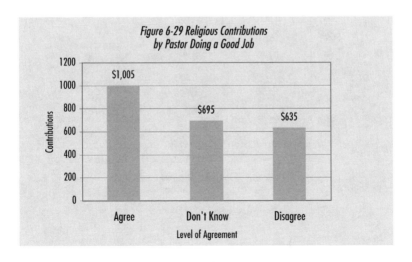

Figure 6-29 Religious Contributions by Pastor Doing a Good Job

The Bottom Line

Finally, we tried to gauge the degree to which Catholics' overall satisfaction with their parish affected their giving. This incorporates their rating of parish programs, their approval of parish decision-making processes, their agreement with any nuances in parish teachings, their sentiments about parish support for a parochial school, their feelings about their pastor, and their relationship with their fellow parishioners into one measure. This is obviously a complicated issue. To capture their attitude toward their parish, we asked them if they would feel a great sense of loss if, for some reason, they had to change parishes. Sixty-four percent either moderately or strongly agreed that they would. If this can be considered a measure of parish commitment, the Catholics in our sample were the least committed to their parish of any of the denominations that we studied. The Lutherans were almost as low (67%), but the others were well over 70%, with the Assemblies of God and Southern Baptists giving their congregations almost an 80% commitment rating.

Does this make a difference in religious contributions? It certainly does. In Figure 6-30 we can see that those who agreed that changing parishes would be a big loss contributed significantly more than those who disagreed or were not sure.

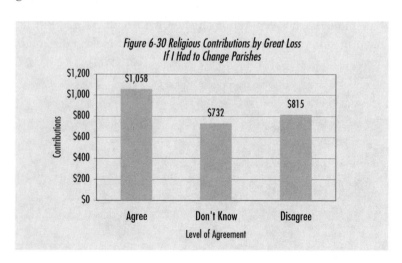

Figure 6-30 Religious Contributions by Great Loss If I Had to Change Parishes

A Word on Priestless Parishes

The vast majority of U.S. Catholic parishes are headed by a resident who serves as the pastor, often assisted by one or more priests serving in the role of parochial vicar, or assistant pastor. But the shortage of priests in the United States (see Schoenherr and Young, 1993) has made it difficult for some dioceses to provide each parish with its own resident priest. These priestless parishes have typically been located in rural areas, although some have been established in inner cities.

A priestless parish is managed by a parish administrator, sometimes referred to as a lay pastor. This is frequently a woman religious, although other laypersons and ordained deacons also serve in this capacity. The parish is served by an ordained priest, who might visit the parish as seldom as once or twice a month. The lay pastor is not allowed to celebrate the Eucharist, instead presiding at Communion services where hosts that were preconsecrated by the visiting priest are distributed. The parish administrator provides many of the services that would be expected of an ordained priest, including preparation for the sacraments. However, the sacraments are administered by the visiting priest, except in those cases where the parish administrator is an ordained deacon. Deacons are authorized to baptize, preside over marriages, and conduct funerals.

As one might expect, there are some problems with priestless parishes (see Gilmour, 1986, and Wallace, 1992). Frequently, a bishop's preparation of a parish for the assignment of a lay pastor has been inadequate. Tensions have arisen because of the role ambiguity between the lay pastor, who is responsible for preparing candidates for sacraments, and the visiting priest, who confers them. There have also been complaints from lay pastors that questions that should have been addressed to them have been inappropriately handled by the visiting priest.

A final problem with priestless parishes has been with the attitude of the parishioners. Some refuse to accept anyone (especially a woman) who serves in a role that they had come to expect would be filled by an ordained male. Also, they may feel that their parish has been downgraded and designated as "second class" if they haven't been assigned a priest on a full-time basis.

This doesn't mean that all priestless parishes are doomed to failure. We should recognize that the skills necessary to be an effective pastor are not automatically conferred at ordination, and many laypersons have been blessed with talents that would make them better pastors than some priests. Also, once a lay pastor has been given the chance to prove herself/himself, any reluctance on the part of parishioners to accept a lay pastor may dissipate.

D'Antonio et al. (1996) found that 55% of their respondents would find it acceptable if their parish structure included a lay parish administrator and a visiting priest. The same survey found that, in the event of a priest shortage, 70% of the respondents would consider Communion services led by laypersons using consecrated hosts to be an acceptable substitute for Sunday Mass (p. 177).

How do priestless parishes affect religious contributions? There were very few priestless parishes in our sample. As Figure 6-31 shows, households in priestless parishes contributed much less to their church than did households in parishes with a resident priest. Unfortunately, because of the small number of priestless parishes in our sample, these differences are not statistically significant. But they are striking, nevertheless.

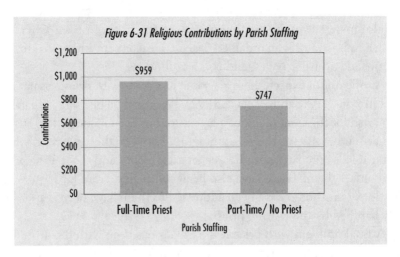

Figure 6-31 Religious Contributions by Parish Staffing

A word of caution is in order — we have a chicken-or-egg problem in interpreting these findings. Are contributions low in priestless parishes because of an absence of a resident priest? Or have these parishes been designated as priestless because of a variety of factors, including low contributions? Our data was not sufficiently detailed to answer these questions; we really need information on contributions before and after the parish was designated as priestless. All we can say for certain is that it appears that parishioners in parishes lacking a resident priest contribute less to their church.

Conclusions About the Role of the Parish

So what can we conclude about the effect of parish-specific factors on Catholic giving? First, contrary to the conventional wisdom, the large size of Catholic parishes is not the overriding factor in explaining low Catholic contributions. It is true that members of large parishes contribute less, but so do members of small parishes. Actually, medium-sized parishes (1,000 to 2,500 members) receive the largest contributions. Factors such as parish programs, liturgies, and preaching also tended not to be important.

Rather, parish decision-making processes tended to be critical in explaining contributions. Parishioners who feel that their parish leadership is accountable and trustworthy in financial matters, who feel that they are a part of the parish financial decision-making process, contribute more. But this desire for lay participation in parish decision-making extends into other areas beyond just parish finances. Parishioners who believe that other types of parish decisions are reached through open processes also contribute more. Clearly, the method of parish decisions being made because "Father said _____" will no longer work.

This is not to say that priests aren't important (parishioners who like their pastor contribute more). What it does mean is that those pastors who lead through a shared decision-making style are likely to be more successful, at least in generating parish contributions, than an autocratic pastor would be.

Parish schools are also important. We're able to confirm Greeley's findings that parishes that sponsor their own parochial schools receive larger contributions. But, curiously, the benefits that a school provides to the parish do not seem to extend to cosponsorship of a consolidated school. Parishes with consolidated schools actually receive lower contributions than do parishes with no school at all. Our findings are also consistent with another of Greeley's findings: parents of parochial school children contribute more than do parents who don't send their children to parochial schools. It might well be, as Greeley asserted, that Catholic schools pay for themselves!

Finally, one of the underlying themes of this book has been the tension between fundraising and stewardship. We've been able to identify factors that would lead to larger contributions without requiring the change in mind-set associated with stewardship. But will the stewardship message work with Catholics? This chapter has shown that the answer is yes. Parishes that deliver a stewardship message receive larger contributions. Concerning the techniques involved in implementing that message, pledging was found to be successful, but other approaches, such as contacting members individually, were not.

Clearly, there are things that can be done at the parish level that will increase contributions without compromising fundamental Catholic Church teachings.

References

Cieslak, Michael J. "Changing Pastors: Does It Lead to a Change in Financial Contributions?" Unpublished paper presented at the 1994 Conference of the Religious Research Association.

_____."Parish Responsiveness and Parish Commitment," *Review of Religious Research*, Vol. 26, No. 2 (December, 1984), pp. 132-47.

Gilmour, Peter. *The Emerging Pastor*. Kansas City: Sheed & Ward, 1986.

Greeley, Andrew, and William McManus. *Catholic Contributions: Sociology and Policy*. Chicago: Thomas More Press, 1987.

Harris, Joseph Claude. "An Analysis of Catholic Sacrificial Giving Programs in Seattle, Washington," *Review of Religious Research*, Vol. 36, No. 2 (December, 1994), pp. 230-37.

Hoge, Dean R., and Boguslaw Augustyn. "Financial Contributions to Catholic Parishes: A Nationwide Study of Determinants," *Review of Religious Research*, Vol. 39, No. 1 (September, 1997), pp. 46-60.

National Conference of Catholic Bishops. "Stewardship: A Disciple's Response," Washington DC: U.S. Catholic Conference, 1993.

Oates, Mary J. *The Catholic Philanthropic Tradition in America*. Bloomington: Indiana University Press, 1995.

Rexhausen, Jeff, and Michael J. Cieslak. "Relationship of Parish Characteristics to Sunday Giving Among Catholics in the Archdiocese of Cincinnati," *Review of Religious Research*, Vol. 36, No. 2 (December, 1994), pp. 218-29.

Schoenherr, Richard A., and Lawrence A. Young. *Full Pews and Empty Altars: Demographics of the Priest Shortage in United States Catholic Dioceses*. Madison: University of Wisconsin Press, 1993.

Wallace, Ruth A. *They Call Her Pastor: A New Role for Catholic Women*. Albany, NY: SUNY Press, 1992.

Welch, Michael R. "Participation and Commitment Among American Catholic Parishioners," in David A. Roozen and C. Kirk Hadaway (Eds.), *Church and Denominational Growth*. Nashville: Abingdon Press, 1993, pp. 324-45.

Zaleski, Peter A., and Charles E. Zech. "Economic and Attitudinal Factors in Catholic and Protestant Religious Giving," *Review of Religious Research*, Vol. 36, No. 2 (December, 1994), pp.158-67.

7

GENERATIONAL DIFFERENCES
IN RELIGIOUS GIVING

This is arguably one of the most contentious times in the history of the U.S. Catholic Church. As the National Pastoral Life Center's document *Called to Be a Catholic* described the situation, "It is widely admitted that the Catholic Church in the United States has entered a time of peril." The document went on to list thirteen issues, including concerns over decision-making and consultation in church governance, the changing roles of women, the shortage of ordained clergy, and dwindling financial support, that caused its authors to reach this conclusion. It referred to "a mood of suspicion and acrimony (that) hangs over many of the most active in the Church's life" (*America*, 1996).

Attempts to understand the basis for these concerns can cut across a variety of dimensions. One popular approach has been Eugene Kennedy's (1995) dichotomy of Culture One and Culture Two Catholics that we described earlier. Briefly, Culture One Catholics view their Catholic faith from an institutional perspective. They place a great deal of reliance on the teaching authority of the Church, whether or not they happen to agree with a specific pronouncement. They actively participate in Church rituals and ceremonies, as well as in debates over the religious controversies of the day. Some might be classified as liberal on these issues, others conservative. But they share an affinity for the Church as an institution. As Kennedy points out, these are the lay Catholics who receive most of the media attention.

In contrast are the Culture Two Catholics. Like Culture One Catholics, Culture Two Catholics identify themselves as Catholic, regularly attend Mass, and recognize a role for the pope and clergy. They are not dissidents. But they place less reliance on the Church as an institution. Rather they look to the Church as a source of meaning as they go about their daily lives. For them the importance of the Church lies not in controversies over the ordination of women or the significance of the latest papal appointment. Rather, the Church's importance lies in the sacramental and pastoral support it provides as they cope with the joys and adversities of everyday life. Theirs is a much more personal, far less institutional, approach to religion.

Although the Kennedy thesis has received a lot of attention, however, it doesn't really get to the issue of discord within the Church. Another dimension, one that perhaps better explains the recent Church unrest, has been identified. This alternative approach views this "suspicion and acrimony" as a product of diverse perspectives held by the distinct generations that populate the U.S. Catholic Church today. According to this theory, the U.S. Catholic Church today consists of three separate generational cohorts, which can be described as follows.

Social scientists have long recognized the importance of "the formative years" in explaining human development. This is the period of late adolescence and young adulthood when social and political attitudes are formed. Some researchers believe the impressionable period starts as young as age 15, while others believe it extends to as late as age 25. Important events (such as the Great Depression, or a war) that individuals experience during their formative years establish their worldviews and have lifelong effects. Each generation shares not only a similar chronological age, but also a perception of society formed by its members' common experiences during their formative years.

Our interest here lies in how the events of individuals' formative period molded their religious attitudes and practices. Applying this theory to Catholic lay persons, the defining religious moment for the various generations of U.S. Catholics was the Second Vatican Council and the reforms that followed. Some Catholics (the pre-Vatican II cohort) experienced their formative years before Vatican II. Another group (the post-Vatican II cohort) was born in the late 1950s and later. Their formative years occurred after the reforms of Vatican II were in place. The middle generation (the Vatican II cohort) was permanently impacted by the occurrence of Vatican II during their formative years. These generations are somewhat analogous to the concepts of pre-baby-boomers, baby-boomers, and Generation X, except that many of those born during World War II would be included in the Vatican II cohort, and the youngest baby-boomers would be combined with the members of Generation X to form the post-Vatican II cohort.

The attitudes of each generation toward religion in general, and specifically, the Catholic Church, are a reflection of both religious and societal occurrences during their formative years. Let's briefly review what some of these influences were and how they affected later religious attitudes.

The pre-Vatican II Cohort

The dominant social events of any Americans who were raised in the 1930s and '40s were first the Great Depression and then World War II. Among the lessons they learned were the importance of cooperation in assisting each other economically and in pulling together to win a war. They came to trust institutional authorities and to rely on them to cope with economic adversity and to bring a peaceful settlement to international conflict. Authority was viewed as promoting the common good (Williams and Davidson, 1996, p. 275).

Catholics of this era tended to be either immigrants or the children of immigrants. They were frequently the victims of religious bigotry. To cope, they joined distinctively Catholic organizations. These organizations emphasized the importance of doctrinal orthodoxy and obeying Church teaching. In the words of Andrea Williams and James Davidson, "Catholics growing up in the 1930s and '40s were socialized into a 'ghetto mentality' which assumed that the world was a hostile place, and that Catholics would be safe if they stayed in the Church and participated in its large array of Catholic organizations. They learned a very collective, institutional approach to faith" (Williams and Davidson, 1996, p. 277).

In summary, pre-Vatican II Catholics were taught to love both their Church and their country. They learned to respect both religious and civil authority.

The Vatican II Cohort

In contrast to the pre-Vatican II generation, Catholics who grew up in the 1950s and '60s experienced two disparate, virtually contradictory eras, both in the secular and religious worlds. In the society at large, the 1950s were characterized by the calm of the Eisenhower administration. Authority and institutions still commanded respect. In contrast, the 1960s were characterized by an unpopular war, assassinations, and racial strife. All authority was questioned and challenged. Confidence in society's institutions diminished as they came to be viewed as part of the problem, not the solution.

By the 1960s, Catholics, riding the wave of the postwar economic expansion, had joined the middle class. They were now integrated into the mainstream of American society. The need for the security offered by the Church and the various Catholic organizations had been mitigated.

Dean Hoge, Benton Johnson, and Donald Luidens chronicled the social and cultural effects that impacted the religiosity of Protestant baby-boomers in their book *Vanishing Boundaries* (1994). Most of these had an effect on Catholic baby-boomers as well. For example, they cited the increase in liberal education among this generation. They argued that liberal education causes religious skepticism and relativism. Likewise, they noted that America had become increasingly pluralistic. The advent of television during this generation's childhood, along with increased travel, had exposed them to other cultures — in this case, cultures beyond the "Catholic ghetto." This could weaken religious beliefs and commitment.

Two other, somewhat similar effects that Hoge et al. recognized were "individualism" and "privatism." The rise of self-centered individualism had weakened churchgoers' ties to their community, including their church. This could result in "faith without community," and leave one with the impression that church attendance and even church authority were optional. Privatism is a closely related concept. It refers to the tendency for Americans to settle in enclaves based on their common socioeconomic characteristics rather than a common history. These lifestyle enclaves value personal fulfillment rather than community. This includes religious beliefs. Religion is considered to be important only to the extent that it contributes to personal fulfillment.

Finally, Hoge et al. recognized the impact on baby-boomers of the change in family structure. Besides the obvious impact of women's growing participation in the workplace, this also included cohabitation before marriage, the rising age of marriage with the corresponding delay in childbirth, and a rising divorce rate. Most religious denominations, not just the Catholic Church, have exhibited an inadequate response to these changes.

Members of this cohort were also exposed to some remarkable changes within the Catholic Church as well. As in the secular world, they are really a part of two different religious eras. In the 1950s, they were raised much like the cohort that preceded them. They learned their religion from the *Baltimore Catechism.* They were taught a very institutional concept of religion: the Catholic Church was the "one true church." The unchallenged following of Church teaching was the only path to heaven.

In the 1960s, all of this changed dramatically. Suddenly, everything was turned upside-down. Rather than viewing the world as a hostile place, Catholics were now told that the Church had to become active in the world. Ecumenism replaced the emphasis on "the one true church." The hierarchical model of the Church was not totally discarded, but the laity was given new respect as "the people of God." They were told that, through their baptism, they shared in the priesthood. They were encouraged to get involved and make their voices heard through parish councils and other lay ministries.

Perhaps of most significance, the institutional emphasis of the Church was replaced by an emphasis on the importance of the individual. Again quoting Williams and Davidson, "At the same time that the Council was telling Catholics that traditions such as Latin Masses and meatless Fridays were no longer important, it was asking them to view their faith in more personal terms. Prior to Vatican II, Catholics were told to look first to the Church for guidance (an 'informed conscience' would be in agreement with Church teaching). The Council placed more emphasis on the integrity of one's conscience" (Williams and Davidson, 1996, p. 278).

This is consistent with the individualism and privatism that Hoge et al. had noted with regards to Protestant baby-boomers.

But the Second Vatican Council wasn't the only earth-shattering religious experience that affected Catholics in the 1960s. In 1968, Pope Paul VI published his encyclical on artificial contraception, *Humanae Vitae*. It's safe to say that the encyclical was not met with unanimous acclaim by either the laity or the clergy. A large portion of married Catholics were already using some form of contraception. The report by the pope's own advisory committee, which had recommended that the birth-control decision be left to the individual couple, had been leaked to the public and had raised expectations about the pope's position. The documents of Vatican II had just declared the supremacy of individual conscience. Not only the laity, but many priests and some bishops, openly dissented with the pope. Some of the dissenting clergy were dealt with harshly. For the first time, many Catholics questioned the teaching authority of the Church (McNamara, 1993, p. 33).

So we see a generational cohort who, during their formative years, was struggling to mesh the respect for authority and institutions that they had learned in the 1950s with the disdain for authority and institutions that had become the hallmark of the 1960s. This was occurring in both their secular and religious lives. One result, as Wade Clark Roof (1993) has pointed out, is that a large portion of them (in fact, two-thirds of the Catholics in his study) dropped out of church at one time or another. Most of those who dropped out did not return. Those who did return were permanently changed. For example, they preferred meditating alone over worshiping with others, and exploring different religions rather than learning more about their own faith.

The post-Vatican II Cohort

The factors that Hoge et al. cited as affecting the religious attitudes of baby-boomers came into full bloom during the formative years of the post-Vatican II generation. In addition, this cohort was raised in an era of cynicism toward both institutions and authority. In the secular world they experienced Watergate and Irangate, which reinforced the suspicion of government that had first emerged during the Vietnam war. They watched as national esteem for the United States' once-vaunted space program collapsed in light of the Challenger explosion and its aftermath. They saw the government seemingly paralyzed by its inability to deal with simultaneously high unemployment and inflation rates. They witnessed their parents or their friends' parents become innocent victims of a wave of corporate downsizing. On a religious level, they were exposed to stories of pedophilia and other misconduct among clergy.

Of course, by this time the reforms of Vatican II were in place. Members of this generation have little direct knowledge of Vatican II, but they have felt its impact. They were not exposed to the *Baltimore Catechism.* Instead, personal responsibility for their own individual faith journey was emphasized. The Church was viewed as a tool for helping them get to heaven, rather than an end in itself. In fact, they likely place more importance on being a good Christian than on being a good Catholic. They feel free to disagree with Church teaching, often distinguishing between God's law and Church law. And they're more likely to consider the specific circumstances before determining the rightness or wrongness of an action (D'Antonio et al., pp. 84-88).

There is plenty of evidence that these different experiences during their impressionable years have had an important effect on the ways in which members of these generational cohorts perceive and practice their religion (see, for example, McNamara, 1993, and Davidson et al., 1997). But have these different experiences systematically affected their religious giving?

To answer this question, we first of all have to specify exactly whom we are including in each cohort. Remember, the data for this study was collected in 1993. Other studies have shown that giving drops off dramatically when people retire. Therefore, we're excluding from this analysis anyone born before 1928. As for the border between the pre-Vatican II cohort and the Vatican II generation, we chose the birth year of 1943. At the other end, we chose the boundary between the Vatican II cohort and the post-Vatican II group as the birth year 1958. We recognize that this latter boundary year is stretching things a bit as to the effect of the changes of the 1960s during their formative years, but we felt that people born in 1958 had more in common with those born before that year than those born after that year. In any event, whatever boundary years we chose would contain some degree of arbitrariness and be open to criticism.

It is also imperative that we recognize that religious giving by these different generations may differ because they are in different stages of their life cycles. The pre-Vatican II group is in their prime earning years, and most don't have to worry about saving to buy a home or to send their children to college. The Vatican II generation, on the other hand, is saving for college, paying off a mortgage, and has yet to reach its best earning years. The post-Vatican II cohort is just beginning, struggling to save for a home or pay a mortgage, starting a family, and earning at or just beyond entry-level incomes. It is no surprise then that, as Figure 7-1 indicates, the pre-Vatican II households in our sample contribute the most, followed by the Vatican II and then the post-Vatican II generations. To account for this in the analysis that follows, we divided each household's contributions by their cohort's average contributions. That allows us to determine whether each determinant that we study leads to above-average or below-average contributions for that cohort by calculating a cohort index. In the figures that follow, a cohort index of 100 indicates giving right at the cohort average. An index less than 100 signifies religious contributions below the cohort average, and a value greater than 100 demonstrates giving at levels above the cohort average.

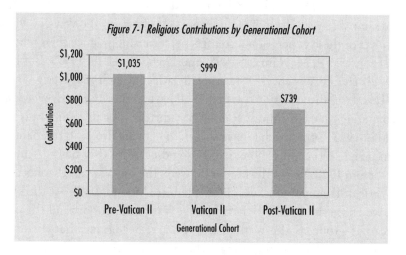

Figure 7-1 Religious Contributions by Generational Cohort

First, we can identify the areas in which there was no significant effect on religious giving. These include the so-called "pelvic" issues (Church teachings on abortion, birth control, and the ordination of women) as well as denominational programs and policies. Members of the different cohorts may not agree with one another on Church teachings, the quality of Church programs, or various Church policies. But their differences did not translate into significant differences in giving across the cohorts.

The results at the parish level were quite different. Here, we found that differences in attitudes among the cohorts resulted in differences in giving in two specific realms: parish decision-making and pledging.

Cohorts and Parish Decision-Making Processes

We saw earlier that parish decision-making processes had a significant effect on giving. In general, we have shown that parishioners who felt that they had both information about and input into parish decisions contributed more. But does this vary by generational cohort? The answer is yes. We asked our sample whether they felt they had enough information about the handling and allocation of parish funds. Figure 7-2 shows that all three cohorts exhibited a drop-off in giving when they were dissatisfied with the amount of financial information that they were given, but the greatest decrease (27%) was experienced by the post-Vatican II group.

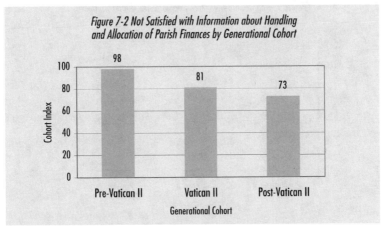

Figure 7-2 Not Satisfied with Information about Handling and Allocation of Parish Finances by Generational Cohort

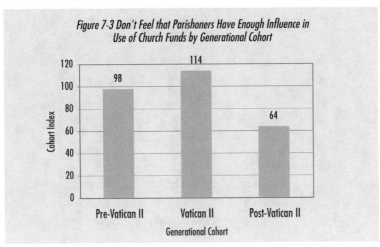

Figure 7-3 Don't Feel that Parishoners Have Enough Influence in Use of Church Funds by Generational Cohort

We had also asked if they thought that typical parishioners had enough influence in parish financial decisions. Among those who indicated that they did not, both the pre-Vatican II group and the post-Vatican II group contributed less than their cohorts' average (actually, a lot less for the post-Vatican II cohort), but the Vatican II group's contributions actually exceeded their cohort's average (Figure 7-3). The pattern of the Vatican II cohort reacting in an opposite fashion from the other two generations is one that occurs frequently, as we'll see throughout this chapter. It is probably symptomatic of the confusion that this cohort feels as a result of its bridging two very different periods in both secular and Church history.

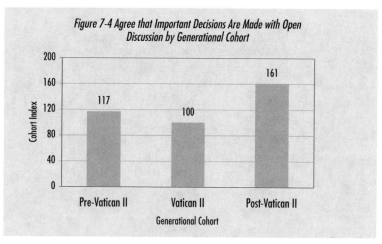

Figure 7-4 Agree that Important Decisions Are Made with Open Discussion by Generational Cohort

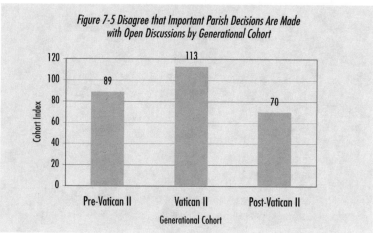

Figure 7-5 Disagree that Important Parish Decisions Are Made with Open Discussions by Generational Cohort

An interesting pattern emerged when we shifted gears and asked about parish decision-making in general. We saw earlier that those who thought that important parish decisions were made after open discussion contributed more. But of that group, the Vatican II generation contributed at just their cohort's average, while the other two groups contributed above their cohort's average (Figure 7-4). In fact, the post-Vatican II group who experienced open discussion in their parish contributed 61% more than the average for their cohort. At the other extreme, those who did not find open discussion in their parish decision-making contributed less. But, as Figure 7-5 shows, when we broke this down by generational cohort, the Vatican II group who did not experience open discussion actually contributed more. The pre-Vatican II group contributed 11% less, and the post-Vatican II group gave 30% less than their respective cohort averages.

What can we conclude about the effect of parish decision-making processes on giving across the three cohorts? First, the Vatican II generation is erratic. Their giving often moves in a pattern counter to the other two cohorts. This could be the result, as mentioned earlier, of confusion among members of this cohort brought about by their bridging of two such dissimilar time periods. The other pattern that emerges is how emphatically open decision-making processes affect the post-Vatican II generation. Their giving drops dramatically (27% to 36% below cohort average) when open processes are not in place, but rises just as dramatically (61% above cohort average) when they are.

Cohorts and Pledging

Earlier we found that members of parishes where pledging is encouraged contribute more. Does this pattern vary by generational cohort? Yes. Figure 7-6 shows that there are significant generational differences in parishes that do not employ pledge cards.

The pre-Vatican II and post-Vatican II cohorts are similar. Their members contribute 22% and 23% less, respectively, than their individual cohort averages. Once again, members of the Vatican II generation are an anomaly as they contribute at a rate slightly above cohort average when their parish doesn't use pledge cards. But for those who disapprove of the practice of pledging, members of all three groups contribute below their respective cohort averages (Figure 7-7). The same is true among those who either

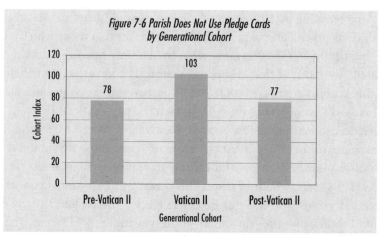

Figure 7-6 Parish Does Not Use Pledge Cards
by Generational Cohort

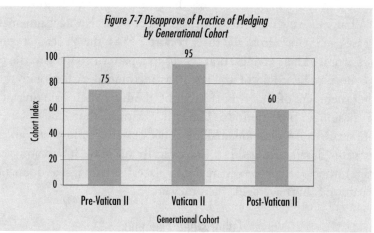

Figure 7-7 Disapprove of Practice of Pledging
by Generational Cohort

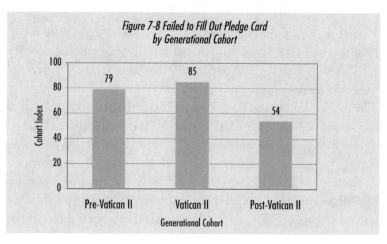

Figure 7-8 Failed to Fill Out Pledge Card
by Generational Cohort

failed to complete a pledge card or weren't certain (Figure 7-8). In both cases, the largest drop-off from average giving in the cohort came with the post-Vatican II generation.

Conclusions

There is strong evidence to support the hypothesis that the U.S. Catholic Church today is populated by three distinct generations. Patrick McNamara (1993) and James Davidson et al. (1997) have convincingly demonstrated that these generational cohorts not only exist, but differ from one another significantly in their religious attitudes and practices. Briefly, the pre-Vatican II generation takes an institutional view towards the Church. When they think of the Church, they think of a hierarchical, authoritarian organization whose primary function is to serve as a mediating force between them and God. They have a great deal of respect for the Church's teaching authority. In contrast, the post-Vatican II cohort views religion as more personal and individualistic. When they think of the Church, they think of themselves. They are the "people of God." They are on a faith journey, and organized religion exists merely to support that journey. They expect a more democratic structure, one in which they are involved in nearly every aspect of Church life. The Vatican II generation is a transition group that has a foot in both camps. They spent their early years in a pre-Vatican II, institutional church, but came of age in a post-Vatican II, individualistic church.

This chapter has shown that many of these differences carry over in their impact on religious giving. In general, we found that the Vatican II generation is unpredictable. Their religious giving frequently is affected in a completely opposite manner than that of other Catholics. Perhaps schizophrenia is too strong a word to use here, but clearly this cohort is far less unified in its thinking than are the members of the other two groups. Given the struggles that we would expect this cohort to have had in trying to blend and make sense of two totally different secular (1950s and 1960s) and religious (pre-Vatican II and post-Vatican II) eras, perhaps this outcome isn't so surprising after all.

Another unexpected trend that we found was the virtually complete agreement between the pre-Vatican II and post-Vatican II cohorts in their giving reactions. The same factors resulted in their giving at levels greater than their cohort average in some instances, and less than their cohort average in others. Having said this, though, we should note that the post-Vatican II cohort exhibited much larger swings in their giving. When factors occurred that they did not approve of (such as the lack of open parish decision-making), their contributions dipped much more than the other groups. But when factors occurred for which they expressed approval (such as the existence of open parish discussion), their giving rose much more rapidly than that of the others.

References

America. "Called to Be Catholic: Church in a Time of Peril," August 31, 1996, pp. 5-8.

D'Antonio, William V., James D. Davidson, Dean R. Hoge, and Ruth A. Wallace. *Laity: American and Catholic.* Kansas City: Sheed & Ward, 1996.

Davidson, James D. et al. *The Search for Common Ground: What Unites and Divides Catholic Americans.* Huntington, IN: Our Sunday Visitor Publishing, 1997.

Hoge, Dean R., Benton Johnson, and Donald A. Luidens. *Vanishing Boundaries.* Louisville: Westminster/John Knox Press, 1994.

Kennedy, Eugene. *Tomorrow's Catholics, Yesterday's Church.* Liguori, MO: Triumph Books, 1995.

McNamara, Patrick. *Conscience First, Tradition Second.* Albany: SUNY Press, 1993.

Roof, Wade Clark. *A Generation of Seekers.* San Francisco: Harper, 1993.

Williams, Andrea S., and James D. Davidson. "Catholic Conceptions of Faith: A Generational Analysis." *Sociology of Religion,* 57 (3): 273-89, 1996.

8

SEVEN THINGS THE CATHOLIC CHURCH CAN DO TO INCREASE CONTRIBUTIONS

In this book I have analyzed a variety of determinants of religious contributions. Some have a significant effect on religious contributions; others do not. Some are within the control of the Church, while others, such as personal characteristics, are not. Of those over which the Church has control, some, because of theological and ecclesiastical reasons, cannot be changed. But that still leaves a broad range of factors that the Church can address if it is serious about increasing parishioners' financial commitments.

The most important activity that a parish can undertake to increase giving is to become a stewardship parish. But stewardship doesn't occur in a vacuum. In order for stewardship to take hold in a parish, a number of other factors must be in place. Otherwise, the stewardship message won't be heard.

The actions that are recommended in this chapter are listed in the sequence that I think they should occur. This sequencing was developed from two sources. The first source was the data presented in the previous chapters. The second source came from insights gathered from discussions with groups to whom the empirical findings had been presented over the years. Since the first printing of this book, I have made presentations based on its findings to a variety of groups. These include numerous presentations at the annual meetings of the International Catholic Stewardship Council; presentations at various diocesan stewardship days; a presentation at an annual meeting of the Diocesan Fiscal Management Conference; and presentations at some parish-level stewardship functions. Each time, I've walked away with a clearer understanding of how stewardship and giving actually come to life in a parish, where the rubber hits the road. In other words, I've learned quite a bit about the "practical theology" of stewardship.

So here are my recommendations, presented in logical sequence. I anticipate that some will disagree with my sequencing. But there should be no controversy over the importance of addressing each of these issues.

1. Build Community

It is a basic axiom of professional fundraisers that people give to people. A parish might be able to raise funds for one-time projects (the organ needs to be replaced, or the roof blew off the church building), but long-term sustained giving relies on the donors feeling a sense of community. If parishioners don't feel a sense of community, the parish shouldn't bother with stewardship. It won't take hold.

The problem is, of course, that Catholic parishes are large. It can be very difficult to build a sense of community in a parish of 4,000 people (a typical-sized parish) or more. But it must be done. The parish needs to find every opportunity to build community. That might include parish-wide programs such as *RENEW* or *Christ Renews His Parish*. It might involve rallying parishioners around a specific cause, such as building a house for Habitat for Humanity or adopting a sister parish. Sponsoring youth events, such as parish sports leagues or Scouts, are effective, although they carry the danger of overlooking parishioners without children. An event like a parish festival, which can involve parishioners from all segments of parish life, is a great way to build community. Whatever approaches a parish takes, it should be aware that community building is a continuous undertaking — it never ends. But in order for parishioners to become more generous, it must begin.

2. Give Parishioners a Role in Parish Decision-Making Processes

We asked the question in a number of different ways, and each time the answer came out the same. Parishioners want more say about how their parishes are run. This extends beyond merely being informed about what's happening. They want to be consulted and have direct input into decision-making processes. In parish financial matters they expect accountability and transparency. This can only be assured when lay people (either directly or through their representation on parish finance committees and parish pastoral councils) have an input into both the development and the approval of the parish budget. The laity also expects to play a role in the nonfinancial matters of the parish. They want open discussion of parish issues. Situations where all decisions are made by the pastor or a small clique of parishioners (either appointed by the pastor or self-appointed) only serve to discourage parishioners, with a predictable effect on their giving.

In many respects, shared parish decision-making is just an extension of stewardship. One effective way of instilling a sense of stewardship in people is to develop in them an attitude of ownership of the resources over which they are stewards. Jesus himself spoke of the relationship between stewardship and ownership/responsibility (Matthew 25:14-30; Luke 19:12-27). It would be difficult to develop a parish of stewards if all parish decision-making has been taken out of their hands. At best, this would leave parishioners with a very incomplete and immature sense of stewardship.

Some would argue that the Catholic Church has a hierarchical, not a congregational, ecclesiology. Most of the parishioners that I have spoken with recognize that, by canon law, the pastor has the final say in all parish decisions. Most parishioners are comfortable with that. All they are asking for is to be consulted, and for there to be transparency and accountability in all parish decisions. If we want them to contribute more money, they would contend, we should be willing to give them some input into the decision-making process, including how that money is spent.

3. Develop Stewardship

The one best thing the Church should do if it is serious about increasing giving among Catholics is to instill a sense of stewardship among its members. This is not only a practical solution, with enormous financial benefits, it is also mission-driven and theologically sound. In fact, stewardship is so much a part of the mission of the Church, so theologically sound, that it probably should be emphasized even if the Church wasn't interested in raising more money. This holistic approach invites renewal at both the individual and parish level.

To be effective, however, it cannot be considered a fringe activity. It has been said that, "The Church is good at developing stewardship programs, but not stewards." Stewardship must be at the center of parish life. Parishes must make significant changes in their orientation. All parish activities and programs need to be evaluated in terms of their impact in developing a community of stewards.

And, as was cautioned earlier, stewardship must go beyond the mere raising of money. The emphases on the time and talent dimensions are at least as critical as the emphasis on treasure. That's why tithing, although it has its advocates, is not one of my suggestions. Because of its narrow focus, tithing does not offer the opportunity for renewal that stewardship does. As an aside, we might note that the value of time contributed to a Church also has a significant monetary value.

Good parish stewardship starts in the parish house. The pastor and the other parish leadership must exhibit good stewardship in their handling of parish resources. They must maintain the highest standards of integrity and honesty in all matters, including the care for parish facilities through preventative maintenance, and using good judgment in making all expenditures. Parishioners who have misgivings concerning the stewardship of their parish leadership can't be expected to develop into good stewards themselves.

This is not the place for a step-by-step guide on how to implement stewardship in the parish. That has already been done, and done very well. Among the best sources of this information are *Stewardship: Disciples Respond*, a guidebook put out by the International Catholic Stewardship Council; *Stewardship: A Parish Handbook* by C. Justin Clements (Liguori Publications); and Paul Wilkes' series "New Beginnings," distributed by St. Anthony Messenger Press.

4. Minimize the Use of "Volunteers"

If we are going to develop the time and talent portions of stewardship, it is important that we impress upon our parishioners that the time and talent that they contribute should be viewed as a "ministry," not merely a "volunteer" activity.

What's the difference? The connotation of being a volunteer is, "It's okay if I do a good job, but it's also okay if I don't. After all, I'm *only* a volunteer." Or, "It's okay if I show up for my commitment, but it's also okay if I don't. After all, I'm *only* a volunteer."

But when parishioners believe that they are engaged in a parish ministry, they know that their activity is vital to the success of the parish. They will take their ministry activity more seriously. As a point of fact, through our baptism, we share in the priesthood of the laity. We are all called to ministry. We have a right and a responsibility to serve as ministers in our parish. Parishioners who serve as lectors, extraordinary ministers of the Eucharist, CCD teachers, members of the parish worship committee, and such are all engaged in a ministry, not a volunteer activity. The parish relies on them to contribute their time and talent.

At the same time, convincing parishioners that they are involved in a ministry, as opposed to a volunteer activity, places a responsibility on the pastor and parish staff. If we want parishioners to treat their activities as a ministry, we need to properly train them, support them, and, yes, hold them accountable. Volunteers don't have high expectations for their training, don't necessarily expect to be supported — and they surely don't expect to be held accountable.

But doing all three conveys the message that our parishioners are involved in a *ministry*, which then makes a profound difference. Evidence shows that when parishioners view their activities as ministries, they will be more dedicated to them, spend more time on them, and — as a happy by-product, because of their heightened involvement — contribute more to support their parish financially. Fr. Thomas Sweetser, the well-regarded parish consultant, has estimated that every time we get a parishioner involved in a *ministry* (rather than a volunteer activity), that parishioner's financial contributions will *double.*

We must recognize the importance of meeting parishioners where they are. Those parishioners who feel that their activities are "only" volunteer activities, not ministry, should not be shunted aside or made to feel guilty. With a little work and attention, we can help them recognize their true roles and value in the ministries of the parish.

5. Institute Pledging

The data from the American Congregational Giving Study reveals that 37% of regular Mass-attending Catholics base their parish contributions on how much they can afford that week. If they can afford more, they contribute more. If they can afford less, they contribute less. If they feel that in that week they can afford nothing at all, or if they miss Mass in their parish for whatever reason, they contribute nothing at all.

On the other hand, those who make a financial commitment to their parish by pledging contribute much more. As we mentioned earlier, pledging was not a very popular concept among participants in our focus groups. But what does it say about a community of people who will make multi-year commitments to purchase automobiles, vacation homes, boats, and the like, but not a yearly commitment to their Church? What do they own, and what owns them? Where are their treasures and their hearts?

Aside from the sound theological arguments for asking people to make a commitment to their Church, the simple truth is that pledging works. People who pledge are better givers. People who plan their religious giving on an annual basis, rather than by looking at their checkbook each Sunday to see what they can afford that week, contribute more. Incidentally, most stewardship programs urge the parish to ask for a commitment of time and talent as well as treasure when their people pledge.

Pledging can be a foreign concept to Catholics and, therefore, difficult to implement. One approach that has been successful in parishes around the country is giving parishioners the option to contribute electronically by having their contributions transferred directly from their checking accounts to the parish. Most Americans now pay at least some of their bills electronically. It makes sense to give them this option for their religious contributions.

Parishioners who commit to electronic withdrawals are in effect, pledging. This means that the parish receives their contributions at the beginning of the month, before other bills are paid (first fruits) and before their checkbook can be depleted. It also means that the parish receives their contributions even if they happen to be out of town, sick, or for whatever reason unable to attend Mass in their home parish on a particular weekend.

Some worry that contributing by electronic transfers undermines the importance of the offertory collection. But the nature of that collection has evolved over the years, from contributions in the form of livestock, to contributions in the form of cash, then to checks. Electronic withdrawals are a natural progression. In fact, the nation's largest collection envelope provider, Our Sunday Visitor, provides envelopes with a check-off box that indicates that the parishioner has contributed electronically. Parishioners using electronic withdrawals drop that envelope in the collection basket along with the envelopes of fellow parishioners that might contain cash or checks. The offertory collection maintains its same liturgical standing.

Good stewardship requires parishioners to make a commitment. The willingness to make a pledge (not only of treasure, but also of time and talent) is an essential part of formalizing that commitment.

6. Meet the Special Needs of Parishioners

Parishes are generally formed around geographic boundaries. In many cases, this means that members have a similar socioeconomic status. But this doesn't mean that a parish should be viewed as a monolith. In many instances their similar socioeconomic status masks a population with diverse needs from their parish. Parishes need to stand ready to meet these needs. Those that are the most successful will probably enjoy larger contributions. Our results show that, while we couldn't single out any one parish program that leads to higher contributions, members who were more satisfied with their parish contributed more.

This is not a particularly startling revelation. But we'd like to point out a few groups that require special parish attention. First, there are the young adults, Generation X and Y, who will soon be the leaders of the Church. We saw in the previous chapter that younger generations have a different set of religious needs and aspirations than earlier generations. As much as parishioners in general want involvement in parish decision-making processes, members of this generation are even more so inclined. This penchant for lay control extends to other aspects of Church life, such as selecting their own pastor. They are more likely to believe in the primacy of individual conscience over Church teachings. To many, it is more important to be a good Christian than it is to be a good Catholic. And, they feel less of an obligation to support their Church financially.

This is a radically different way of thinking about the Catholic Church. It is a permanent shift in attitude, not just a "stage" that they are going through. It is important that the Church make whatever adjustments it can, within theologically acceptable limits, to accommodate this cohort. The impact of this cohort's approach to religion extends far beyond mere financial implications. Like stewardship, this is such an important issue that it would need to be addressed even if there were no financial benefits at stake. But the fact that this cohort will be the primary financial supporters of the Church throughout the first half of this century only serves to make it more critical.

Another group that warrants special attention are the adult parishioners (single, widowed, and divorced or separated) who do not have children living at home. These households are among the Church's better givers, but they are often forgotten as parishes gear their programs and resources towards children.

Finally, every study has concluded that, while Catholics contribute less than most Protestant denominations, the gap between Protestant and Catholic giving grows as household income increases, and the gap is greatest among our wealthiest Catholics. Somehow, we have failed this group. We have failed to teach them the joy of giving. We have failed to assist them in the conversion of their minds and hearts. We need to carve out a special message (without providing them privileged status) that will convey the stewardship message to our wealthiest Catholics.

7. Remind Parishioners that Contributing Through Estate Planning is Good Stewardship

As the baby-boomer generation approaches retirement age, one of their priorities becomes saving enough money for retirement. No one knows for sure how long he or she will live, or how much anyone will need to have saved to ensure a comfortable retirement. As a result, their financial contributions to their Church as they approach retirement age might fall short of their actual ability to contribute. They might not be as good stewards as they could be.

In many cases, it will turn out that once they die, they will have saved more than was needed. A wonderful way to make up for any shortfall in their stewardship of treasure while they were alive is to remember the Church in a bequest. Contributing to the Church through estate planning is not only good stewardship; it frequently offers the estate significant tax savings as well.

Conclusion

Throughout this book, there has run an undercurrent of tension between the theological message of stewardship and the practical elements of fundraising. In many ways, the two *are* at odds. Fundraising is what we do; stewardship is who we are. Fundraising is one-dimensional, impacting only people's checkbooks; stewardship invites us to change our hearts. Fundraising typically occurs annually, in conjunction with financing the parish budget; stewardship is an ongoing commitment.

By placing stewardship as our number-one recommendation, it should be clear to the reader where we stand on this issue. Yet, we recognize a role for both. It is difficult for us to imagine a successful stewardship campaign, no matter how well thought out or theologically grounded, occurring in a parish where the parishioners don't feel a sense of community; where the laity isn't a part of the decision-making process; where they take on a volunteer, rather than a ministry, attitude towards their activities in the parish; where they are unwilling to make a commitment to their parish; and where the needs of the individual segments of the parish are not being met.

In short, these other recommendations — which resonate with a fundraising message — should be viewed as preconditions to successful parish stewardship. Stewardship is primary, but without these other factors in place, any stewardship program will at a minimum be less effective than it could be, and may even be doomed to failure.

References

Zech, Charles E., Patrick McNamara, and Dean R. Hoge. "Lagging Stewards, Part Two: Catholics as Church Volunteers," *America*, February 8, 1997, pp. 21-25.

ADDENDUM

In the process of updating *Why Catholics Don't Give... And What Can Be Done About It* for this second edition, it was impossible for me to ignore the most important issue to concern the Catholic Church in recent memory — the clergy sexual abuse scandal. The scandal has not only affected those directly involved, including obviously both victims and perpetrators, but also many others who love the Church. Some have been horrified by stories of bishops and others in responsible positions who continually protected and reassigned known abusers. Others, though saddened by the tales of abusive priests and helpless victims, believed that bishops and others made honest mistakes based on the best information available to them at the time, and that the whole episode has been blown out of proportion by an anti-Catholic media. Nearly every parishioner has had an opinion on the scandal and the way it has been handled.

The scandal has the potential to significantly affect giving to the Church. The impact can be seen in both its short-term effects and long-term implications. In the short term, we might expect two different reactions. Some Catholics will likely increase their contributions in a show of support for their pastor and Church leaders and to continue the work of the Church. Others might take the opposite approach and show their displeasure with the Church leadership and its handling of the scandal by decreasing, or even discontinuing, their financial support of the Church.

There are numerous potential long-term repercussions. Some parishioners have expressed the opinion that revelations related to the scandal call for the Church to be more financially accountable and transparent. Some dioceses, under the weight of the burden of the financial settlements associated with this scandal, have been forced to develop innovative ways of raising funds. One approach that was used in some dioceses was to close parishes in order to save money. Other dioceses chose to declare bankruptcy, with all of its uncharted legal ramifications.

In an effort to learn more about these and other possible impacts on Catholic giving, I was fortunate enough to be invited to participate in a series of nationwide studies of Catholic parishioner attitudes that was funded by FADICA (Foundations and Donors Interested in Catholic Activities, Inc.). FADICA is a consortium of private charitable foundations and individual donors who share an interest in religious philanthropy. They commissioned three nationwide polls of U.S. Catholic parishioner opinions on the scandal and its aftermath as it relates to Catholic giving.

The first poll was conducted in the fall of 2002 by the Gallup organization as news of the scandal and all of its aspects were first unfolding. The latter two polls were conducted by Zogby International. One was conducted in the fall of 2004 and the other in the fall of 2005. Both of these polls examine opinions after parishioners have had the opportunity to reflect on the ramifications of the scandal.

Each survey interviewed 1000 randomly selected Catholics. As with most surveys of this type (including the survey that served as the basis for this book) this sample is biased. The vast majority of those who chose to complete the survey are regular Mass-attending Catholics. In each of the survey years, more than 70% of the respondents indicated that they attend Mass at least weekly. While this bias presents some unease for social scientists who prefer a bias-free sample, it gives the results about to be reported some degree of credibility. For the most part, these are not the opinions of disaffected Catholics who only attend Mass twice a year. These are the opinions of the regular Mass attendees, the folks that we see in the pews week in and week out. These are our most dedicated Catholics speaking.

In the sections that follow, I will present the findings on the short-term giving issues and the long-term ramifications separately.

Short-Term Effects

The primary short-term effect is on parishioners' decisions to contribute to support the Church financially. Catholics are asked to support the work of the Church on three levels:

- They support their parish through the regular Sunday Offertory collection.
- They support the work of diocesan programs through their contributions to Catholic Charities or, as in some dioceses, by contributing to the Bishop's Annual Appeal.
- They fund the work of the Church nationwide and worldwide by contributing to the collections endorsed by the United States Conference of Catholic Bishops. These include such collections as those that finance the Catholic Campaign for Human Development, Aid to Central and Eastern Europe, and the National Religious Retirement Office.

How did the scandal and its aftermath affect giving at each of these levels? Figures A-1 to A-3 show the percent of respondents in each year of the surveys who either contributed more or who chose to contribute less or discontinue giving altogether at each level of Church giving.

Before we analyze the findings contained in Figures A-1 to A-3, a couple of caveats are in order. First, the figures represent the number of givers, not the dollar amounts contributed. Religious giving is frequently characterized by the 20/80 rule — 20% of the parishioners contribute 80% of the funds. In fact, further analysis of the data reveals that most of those in our sample who had responded to the scandal by either giving less or nothing at all had been low givers to begin with. A large portion of those in the sample who were contributing more had previously been generous givers. This is consistent with anecdotal evidence that indicated that in the wake of the scandal, nationwide at each level of giving the number of donors was down, but the actual dollar amounts contributed had held steady or suffered only a modest decline.

Second, the proportion of Catholics who regularly attend Sunday Mass has been in decline for some time now. Studies, such as the annual poll conducted by CARA (Center for Applied Research in the Apostolate) have shown that the scandal did not accelerate the decline, but it certainly did not halt it. Even if individual Catholic contributions had held steady, the Church might have suffered a decline in overall contributions.

Third, there are a variety of reasons why individuals would increase or decrease their donations to the Church. We didn't ask the reason for any change in 2002; we did ask in 2004 and 2005. In 2004, the largest number,

37 percent, told us that their decision to financially support the Church was driven by the recognition that the Church needs their contributions. The second most important factor was the state of the economy, which was mentioned by 20% of the respondents. Of those responses that were related to the scandal, 9% simply cited the scandal, 6% alluded to concerns about Church financial accountability issues, and 6% listed unfair treatment that the Church had received in the secular press.

In 2005, of those who increased their giving, the primary reason given was the recognition that the Church needs their financial support to carry out its ministries (36%), followed by a change in their personal financial situation (34%). Other frequently cited reasons for increased giving included the importance of stewardship to the respondent (14%) and overall satisfaction with the Church/bishop/pastor (10%).

Of those who had decreased or discontinued their contributions to the Church, the primary reason given was continued anger over the scandal (40%), followed by a worsening of their personal financial situation (27%). Other frequently cited reasons for a decrease/discontinuation of giving included an overall dissatisfaction with the Church/bishop/pastor (13%) and concerns over the lack of accountability in Church finances (7%).

Having said this, a few patterns emerge from the data in Figures A-1 to A-3:

- Initially, at each level of giving, those who gave less or stopped giving substantially outnumbered those who contributed more.
- At each level of giving, the gap between the number of respondents in each group has narrowed over time, and in the case of parish giving, the number of respondents who increased their giving eventually surpassed the number who were giving less/nothing.
- The smallest number of respondents who decreased or discontinued their giving — and the largest number who increased their giving — came at the parish level. As other polls have shown (including the one supporting this book), most parishioners have a very favorable impression of their pastor and like their parish. Most were reluctant to punish their parish if there had no direct parish involvement in the scandal. Rather, parishioners tended to hold their bishop, and especially the USCCB, accountable for the scandal and its after-

math by significantly reducing their contributions at the diocesan and national levels. As noted, this pattern has moderated.

So, what can we conclude about the short-run impact of the scandal on parishioners' decisions to support the Church financially? Clearly, there was an immediate effect on giving at all levels to the Church. Those who decreased or discontinued their giving outnumbered those who had increased their donations by a wide margin at all levels of Church giving. The impact probably varied by location, with a greater decrease in giving occurring in dioceses most involved in the scandal and its aftermath.

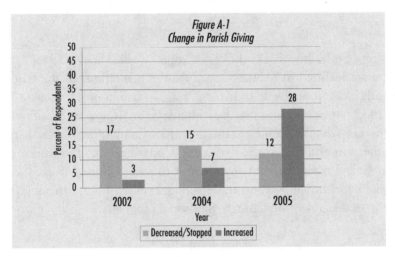

Figure A-1
Change in Parish Giving

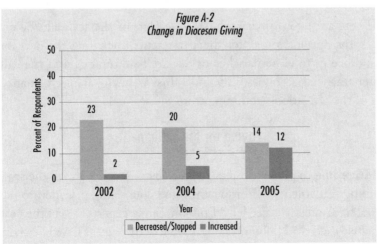

Figure A-2
Change in Diocesan Giving

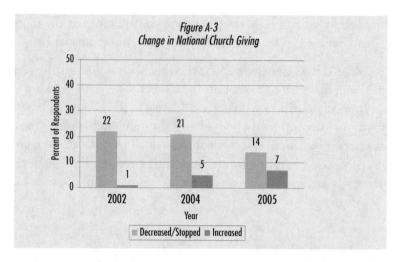

Figure A-3
Change in National Church Giving

Apparently, though, the short-run impact is subsiding, as fewer parishioners are inclined to reduce or stop their contributions to the Church, and others are more likely to increase their contributions. Evidence from our 2005 survey indicates that parishioner giving is now more influenced by the household's financial situation than its opinion of the scandal. Another important factor is that many Catholics value the work of the Church, and recognize that any attempt to punish those involved in the scandal by withholding contributions might only wind up harming those who were dependent on Church-sponsored programs.

Long-Term Effects

There are two primary long-term effects of the scandal: the choice among the options to pay for the settlements (including the decision by some dioceses to close parishes or declare bankruptcy), and the call for greater financial accountability and transparency of Church finances in light of the revelations stemming from the scandal.

Paying for the Settlements

According to published reports, the costs associated with the scandal, including settlements paid to victims and counseling provided to perpetrators, have already exceeded $1 billion. Some experts expect the costs to ultimately exceed $2 billion. Though some of these costs have been covered by insurance, many dioceses have been forced to scramble to raise the funds necessary to finance the remainder.

We asked our respondents in both 2004 and 2005 about their view of acceptable options to pay for the scandal once insurance coverage had been exhausted. They were allowed to select more than one option. The results are shown in Figure A-4.

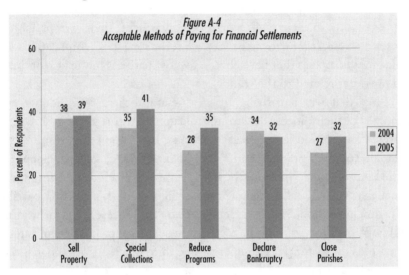

Figure A-4
Acceptable Methods of Paying for Financial Settlements

As expected, one of the more popular options was to sell diocesan property. In fact, Figure A-4 probably understates the popularity of this option. In 2005 we gave our respondents the opportunity to add other options to the list that we had provided. Another 4% added "sell financial assets."

The option of reducing diocesan programs received only modest support, which was somewhat of a surprise. But an even bigger surprise was the backing received by the other three options.

In 2004, more than a third of the respondents favored a special diocesan-wide collection, with the funds directed solely to pay expenses associated with the scandal. In 2005, this figure rose to more than 40%. While parishioners clearly would be unhappy to learn that their regular contributions to the Church had been used to surreptitiously pay for the costs associated with the scandal, many would be willing to contribute to a special collection designated for that purpose. This indicates an underlying layer of good will on the part of parishioners. Many recognize that, although mistakes have been made in the past, the Church needs their support now. They are willing to provide it.

Another surprise was the number of respondents who supported closing parishes to raise funds to pay for the scandal. More than a quarter of the respondents in 2004 thought that this was acceptable, increasing to almost a third in 2005. There might be a bit of a NIMBY (Not In My Backyard) mentality here. Some parishioners would not object to the closing of parishes in theory, but would be very upset if their own parish was chosen to close. It remains to be seen what the long-term implications will be for those dioceses that have chosen to close parishes in the face of financial pressures related to the scandal.

Finally, it was surprising to see the number of respondents who approved of their diocese declaring bankruptcy. At this writing, three U.S. dioceses have found it necessary to declare bankruptcy as a result of the scandal: Tucson, Spokane, and Portland (OR). One, Tucson, essentially settled out of court. Spokane is currently appealing a judge's ruling to the effect that virtually all Church property in a diocese, including parishes and parochial schools, are in effect owned by the diocese. This means that, in theory, the diocese could be required to sell these properties in order to raise funds to pay for the settlements. The third diocese, Portland, has only recently had its initial hearing with regards to its bankruptcy filing.

In both 2004 and 2005, we asked our respondents about a possible impact on their giving if their diocese was to declare bankruptcy. The results are shown in Figure A-5.

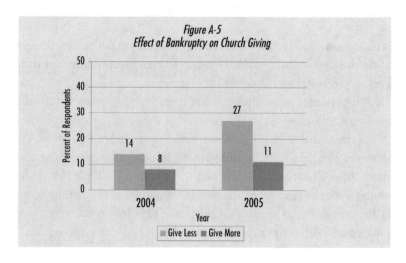

Figure A-5
Effect of Bankruptcy on Church Giving

Surprisingly, while some parishioners would increase their contributions, many more would decrease their giving if their diocese declared bankruptcy. This pattern was exacerbated in the 2005 survey, which was taken after the initial court decision on the Spokane case. Unfortunately, we neglected to ask our sample the reasons behind their opinion. We can only speculate. Perhaps they were influenced by news reports concerning the Spokane bankruptcy case and worried that their parish contributions would wind up paying for the settlements.

In conclusion, over the long-term, regular Mass-attending Catholics show a varying level of support for a variety of options for paying for the settlements associated with the scandal. Selling diocesan property and reducing diocesan programs are obvious components of any plan to raise funds for this purpose. Somewhat surprising is the level of support that parishioners showed for a special diocesan-wide collection, with the funds specifically designated to expenses related to the scandal. The long-term effects of the two most dramatic options, closing parishes and declaring bankruptcy, remain to be seen.

Financial Accountability and Transparency

In the original survey that supported the body of this book, regular Mass-attending Catholics made it clear that Church financial accountability and transparency were important issues to them, and reflected in their decision to donate funds to the Church. If anything, the scandal has intensified this sentiment. Catholics learned that in the past funds for victim settlements and perpetrator counseling had been routinely paid out in some dioceses. Many believe that, with greater financial oversight, these payouts would have exposed the problem and perhaps diminished it before it had reached scandalous proportions.

In each year of our recent surveys, we asked about Church financial accountability. In 2004 and 2005, we also asked whether parishioners had an adequate understanding of how their contributions are used. The responses of our sample of regular Mass-attending Catholics are shown in Figures A-6 to A-8.

In Figure A-6, we see that a minority (and a declining percent over time) rate the bishops as above average in their financial accountability. Figure A-7 reinforces this concern by showing that about two-thirds of

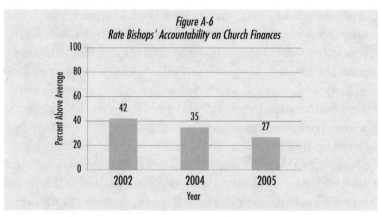

Figure A-6
Rate Bishops' Accountability on Church Finances

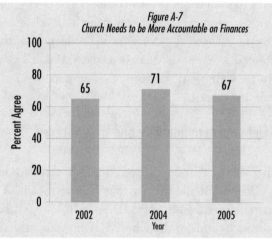

Figure A-7
Church Needs to be More Accountable on Finances

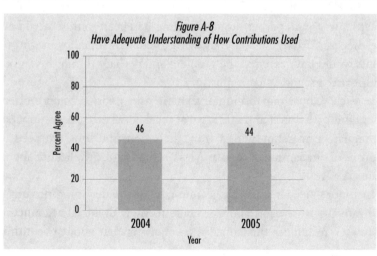

Figure A-8
Have Adequate Understanding of How Contributions Used

regular Mass-attending Catholics agree that the Church needs to be more accountable in its finances. Figure A-8 reveals that fewer than half of our sample believes that they have an adequate understanding of how their contributions are used.

So, how to proceed? One suggestion that has been put forward is to have the Church undergo independent audits at every level, with the results to be released publicly. This can be expensive, especially if we are to audit every parish every year, but it might be necessary to restore parishioners' confidence in the Church's handling of their contributions. Our sample of regular Mass-attending Catholics found this to be an attractive option, as shown in Figure A-9.

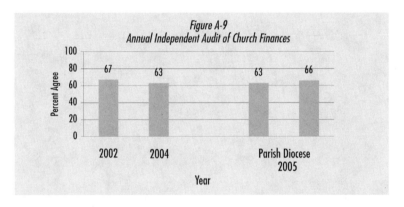

Figure A-9
Annual Independent Audit of Church Finances

In both 2002 and 2004 we asked our respondents about their opinions of independent audits in general. In 2005, we specifically asked about audits at the parish and diocesan levels. In all cases, a solid majority of our samples supported the notion of auditing Church finances and releasing the information publicly.

Another proposal that might inspire parishioners to have more confidence in the Church's handling of money is for parishes to be more open in their finances. In 2004 and 2005, we asked our respondents about their opinion of open forums to discuss parish finances. In both years, approximately 80% of our sample of regular Mass-attending Catholics approved of this approach.

In conclusion, some have speculated that ultimately, the primary long-term outcome of the scandal will be its impact on Church finances and parishioners' willingness to contribute. Church leaders need to be extremely careful over the next few years. Their decisions on the best methods for paying for the scandal (close parishes? declare bankruptcy?) as well as their willingness to become more financially accountable and transparent may well determine the Church's financial wherewithal well into the middle of this century.

APPENDIX A

RESPONSES TO CONGREGATION PROFILES

This appendix gives the percentage responses to the items asked in the Congregation Profiles. There were 125 congregations in each denomination. All the data were weighted to represent a random sample of congregations in each denomination. Columns may not total to 100 because of rounding.

(Q1 concerned the specific denominations of individual respondents.)

Q2. When was the congregation founded?

	AOG	SBC	CATH	LUTH	PRES
Before 1900	0	34	36	47	57
1900-1949	36	26	33	15	21
1950-1979	36	28	29	35	19
1980 or later	28	12	2	3	3

Q3. Which of the following best describes the pastoral staff situation of your congregation during the last complete fiscal year?

	AOG	SBC	CATH	LUTH	PRES
At least one full-time pastor	95	89	93	84	87
Part-time pastor	5	9	7	13	13
Position temporarily vacant	1	3	0	4	0

Q4. Number of members

	AOG	SBC	CATH	LUTH	PRES
1 to 100	32	22	0	16	26
101 to 250	37	41	6	40	35
251 to 500	20	20	10	30	25
501 to 1,000	8	14	16	10	10
1,001 to 2,500	4	4	26	4	4
2,501 to 5,000	0	1	23	0	1
5,001 to 10,000	0	0	18	0	0

(Q5 dealt specifically with Assembly of God churches, omitted here.)

Q6. Number of households

	AOG	SBC	CATH	LUTH	PRES
1 to 100	74	57	7	42	43
101 to 250	19	23	13	42	42
251 to 500	3	14	20	12	10
501 to 1,000	3	5	22	2	4
1,001 to 2,500	1	1	29	2	1
2,501 to 5,000	0	0	9	0	1
5,001 to 10,000	0	0	1	0	0

Q7. What was the average worship attendance on a typical weekend? Give total for all worship services. Persons attending more than once should be counted only once.

	AOG	SBC	CATH	LUTH	PRES
1 to 100	50	53	3	51	52
101 to 250	37	31	9	34	35
251 to 500	8	12	15	13	10
501 to 1,000	5	4	25	2	3
1,001 to 2,500	1	1	36	0	1
2,501 to 5,000	0	0	10	0	0
5,001 to 10,000	0	0	1	0	0

Q8. Where is your congregation located?

	AOG	SBC	CATH	LUTH	PRES
Large city (over 250,000)	18	16	15	13	21
Suburb of large city	14	13	9	8	20
Medium city (under 250,000)	14	8	12	12	9
Suburb of medium city	3	2	5	5	3
Small city (10,000 to 49,000)	24	10	22	12	13
Town (2,500 or more)	14	8	20	12	14
Town (2,500 or less)	5	12	14	18	14
Rural	9	32	4	20	7

Q9. What percent of your members are female?

	AOG	SBC	CATH	LUTH	PRES
0 - 20	0	0	0	0	0
21 - 40	0	3	1	2	2
41 - 60	73	76	93	85	66
61 - 80	27	20	6	11	32
81 - 10	0	0	1	0	2

Q10. Age:

18 – 24 years old

	AOG	SBC	CATH	LUTH	PRES
0- 20	83	95	922	95	95
21 - 40	16	4	8	5	6
41 - 60	1	1	0	0	0

25 – 39 years old

	AOG	SBC	CATH	LUTH	PRES
0 - 20	21	38	42	38	38
21 - 40	58	52	55	58	56
41 - 60	14	9	2	4	6
61 - 80	6	2	1	0	1
81 - 100	1	0	0	0	0

60 – 75 years old

	AOG	SBC	CATH	LUTH	PRES
0 - 20	76	52	61	45	41
21 - 40	20	41	33	47	48
41 - 60	5	6	4	8	11
61 - 80	0	1	1	0	0

>75 years old

	AOG	SBC	CATH	LUTH	PRES
0 - 20	99	93	95	90	81
21 - 40	1	7	5	10	16
41 - 60	0	0	0	0	3

Q11. What percent of your members are:

African-American

	AOG	SBC	CATH	LUTH	PRES
0 - 20	97	96	99	99	93
21 - 40	1	0	0	0	3
41 - 60	0	0	0	1	0
61 - 80	0	0	0	0	0
81 - 100	2	4	1	0	4

Asian

	AOG	SBC	CATH	LUTH	PRES
0 - 20	99	100	97	100	100
21 - 40	1	0	1	0	0
61 - 80	0	0	1	0	0

Hispanic

	AOG	SBC	CATH	LUTH	PRES
0 - 20	88	99	91	100	99
21 - 40	4	1	5	0	1
41 - 60	1	0	2	0	0
61 - 80	1	0	0	0	0
81 - 100	7	0	2	0	0

Native American

	AOG	SBC	CATH	LUTH	PRES
0 - 20	99	97	100	96	100
21 - 40	1	0	0	0	0
41 - 60	0	0	0	0	0
61 - 80	0	1	0	0	0
81 - 100	0	0	2	0	1

White

	AOG	SBC	CATH	LUTH	PRES
0 - 20	10	7	6	1	4
21 - 40	1	0	1	0	0
41 - 60	3	0	4	1	0
61 - 80	7	4	5	2	4
81 - 100	79	89	84	97	92

Others

	AOG	SBC	CATH	LUTH	PRES
0 - 20	99	100	100	100	100
21 - 40	1	0	0	0	0
41 - 60	0	0	0	0	0
61 - 80	0	0	0	0	0
81 - 100	1	0	0	0	0

Q12. What percent of your members have:

College degree

	AOG	SBC	CATH	LUTH	PRES
0 - 20	69	54	41	51	24
21 - 40	20	27	40	26	24
41 - 60	9	12	14	9	25
61 - 80	2	7	6	13	19
81 - 100	0	1	0	1	9

High-school diploma

	AOG	SBC	CATH	LUTH	PRES
0 - 20	6	6	3	3	15
21 - 40	8	13	19	17	24
41 - 60	18	25	62	23	29
61 - 80	40	43	31	47	25
81 - 100	28	13	7	11	8

<High-school diploma

	AOG	SBC	CATH	LUTH	PRES
0 - 20	85	79	87	83	95
21 - 40	9	14	10	15	4
41 - 60	1	3	3	1	0
61 - 80	5	3	0	1	1
81 - 100	0	1	0	0	0

Q13. What percent of your members would you estimate have household incomes of:

<20,000

	AOG	SBC	CATH	LUTH	PRES
0 - 20	50	57	56	52	67
21 - 40	21	21	28	30	14
41 - 60	13	9	8	11	8
61 - 80	8	8	7	5	9
81 - 100	8	6	1	3	3

20,000 - 50,000

	AOG	SBC	CATH	LUTH	PRES
0 - 20	11	10	8	8	8
21 - 40	14	18	19	22	24
41 - 60	30	23	38	37	34
61 - 80	29	40	28	29	28
81 - 100	16	10	8	5	6

50,000 - 100,000

	AOG	SBC	CATH	LUTH	PRES
0 - 20	89	78	71	68	59
21 - 40	9	19	23	25	86
41 - 60	1	3	5	6	11
61 - 80	1	1	1	1	2

>100,000

	AOG	SBC	CATH	LUTH	PRES
0 - 20	100	100	100	100	97
21 - 40	0	0	0	0	3

Q14. What organized groups did your congregation sponsor last year?

	AOG	SBC	CATH	LUTH	PRES
Children Sunday school	98	99	99	94	97
Youth Sunday school	92	99	90	84	90
Adult Sunday school	98	100	53	79	87
Prayer group (church)	95	95	65	66	75
Prayer group (home)	43	23	30	43	35
Singles' group	24	30	14	5	10
Men's groups	58	54	57	24	36
Women's group	84	82	81	90	93
Senior adults' group	31	47	45	32	48
Youth group	92	81	75	64	79
Children's group	91	70	47	39	49
Music program	55	58	34	37	52
Other	52	65	34	27	43

Q15. Did your congregation operate a parochial (five-day-a-week) school last year? (Do not include day-care center, preschool, or before-or after-school "latchkey" programs.)

	AOG	SBC	CATH	LUTH	PRES
Yes	8	0	39	2	1
No	92	0	61	98	99

Q16. Did your congregation cosponsor, with other congregations, a parochial school?

	AOG	SBC	CATH	LUTH	PRES
Yes	2	0	30	0	0
No	98	100	70	100	100

Q17. Did your congregation sponsor a day care center or preschool?

	AOG	SBC	CATH	LUTH	PRES
Yes	9	10	35	18	30
No	92	91	65	82	70

Q18. Did your congregation sponsor a before- or after-school "latchkey" program?

	AOG	SBC	CATH	LUTH	PRES
Yes	5	3	21	6	9
No	96	97	79	94	91

Q19. Is space in your facility used, rent-free, for any community social programs?

	AOG	SBC	CATH	LUTH	PRES
Yes	34	42	75	76	81
No	66	58	25	24	19

Q20. Did your congregation sponsor or support at least one missionary last year?

	AOG	SBC	CATH	LUTH	PRES
Yes	97	52	66	30	54
No	3	48	34	70	46

Q21A. For the last complete fiscal year, how much money came from the following?

Income — regular offerings

	AOG	SBC	CATH	LUTH	PRES
<50,000	22	26	12	32	24
50,001 - 100,000	39	35	16	29	28

100,001 - 200,000	24	24	16	27	29
200,001 - 500,000	11	10	42	10	13
>500,000	4	6	14	1	6

Q21B. Income — special offerings

	AOG	SBC	CATH	LUTH	PRES
0 - 2,000	42	18	10	34	21
2,001 - 5,000	13	14	17	18	20
5,001 - 10,000	10	16	25	14	19
10,001 - 25,000	20	26	49	14	18
>25,000	16	26	51	21	22

Q21C. Income — special fundraisers

	AOG	SBC	CATH	LUTH	PRES
0 - 100	61	82	35	56	62
101 - 500	8	2	2	7	11
501 - 1,000	8	5	4	6	6
1,001 - 2,500	7	4	8	17	5
2,501 - 5,000	7	4	5	9	7
5,001 - 10,000	6	1	8	3	6
>10,000	4	2	38	4	3

Q21D. Income — wills, bequests, and special gifts

	AOG	SBC	CATH	LUTH	PRES
0 - 100	80	77	39	46	54
101 - 500	8	2	6	7	7
501 - 1,000	1	3	4	3	2
1,001 - 2,500	3	1	9	11	8
2,501 - 5,000	3	5	6	9	7
5,001 - 10,000	3	4	30	14	16

Q21E. Income — investments

	AOG	SBC	CATH	LUTH	PRES
0 - 100	84	74	36	40	24
101 - 500	5	8	4	14	12
501 - 1,000	3	5	8	7	8
1,001 - 2,500	3	4	16	13	20
2,501 - 5,000	1	4	8	9	11

5,001 - 10,000	3	1	10	8	12
>10,000	1	5	18	10	15

Q21F. Income — rents and fees

	AOG	SBC	CATH	LUTH	PRES
0 - 100	80	84	49	53	46
101 - 500	1	4	5	5	10
501 - 1,000	1	1	4	8	4
1,001 - 2,500	1	1	10	9	7
2,501 - 5,000	6	7	13	11	13
5,001 - 10,000	5	1	8	7	10
>10,000	7	3	10	7	11

Q21G. Income — judicatory subsidies

	AOG	SBC	CATH	LUTH	PRES
0 - 100	97	97	86	92	88
101 - 500	1	1	0	0	3
501 - 1,000	0	0	2	2	0
1,001 - 2,500	0	0	3	1	1
2,501 - 5,000	1	0	3	0	1
>10,000	1	2	4	2	4

Q21H. Income — other

	AOG	SBC	CATH	LUTH	PRES
0 - 100	87	94	60	77	76
101 - 500	2	1	1	5	0
501 - 1,000	1	2	1	2	1
1,001 - 2,500	2	2	5	7	6
5,001 - 10,000	1	1	10	2	3
>10,000	6	1	14	3	7

Q21I. Total income

	AOG	SBC	CATH	LUTH	PRES
<50,000	18	22	8	20	14
50,001 - 100,000	31	31	11	28	23
100,001 - 200,000	30	24	17	32	31
200,001 - 500,000	17	14	36	17	23
>500,000	4	9	29	3	9

Q22. Capital campaign last year?

	AOG	SBC	CATH	LUTH	PRES
Yes	25	26	22	29	36
No	75	74	78	71	64

Q23A. Congregation have endowment?

	AOG	SBC	CATH	LUTH	PRES
No	97	84	17	42	44
Yes	3	16	83	58	56

Q23B. Amount of endowment

	AOG	SBC	CATH	LUTH	PRES
<50,000	97	91	57	61	64
50,001 - 100,000	2	6	11	21	5
100,001 - 250,000	2	4	17	15	16
250,001 - 500,000	0	0	12	0	8
>500,000	0	0	3	4	8

Q23C. Use of endowment income

	AOG	SBC	CATH	LUTH	PRES
General operating budget	1	4	3	18	23
Capital improvement	1	8	3	20	20
Special programs	0	5	3	21	21
Other	0	7	8	14	9

Q24A. Congregation expenses — operations

	AOG	SBC	CATH	LUTH	PRES
<50,000	24	30	8	24	15
50,001 - 100,000	33	29	17	30	27
100,001 - 200,000	26	20	21	29	30
200,001 - 500,000	12	15	39	15	21
>500,000	4	6	14	3	7

Q24B. Expenses — school subsidies

	AOG	SBC	CATH	LUTH	PRES
0 - 100	91	99	31	94	90
101 - 500	1	0	1	0	1
501 - 1,000	1	0	0	1	2
1,001 - 2,500	1	1	4	0	1
2,501 - 5,000	1	0	0	1	2
5,001 - 10,000	2	0	7	4	1
>10,000	4	1	55	0	1

Q24C. Expenses — denominational program

	AOG	SBC	CATH	LUTH	PRES
0 - 100	3	0	1	2	1
101 - 500	4	2	0	0	1
501 - 1,000	4	2	1	5	3
1,001 - 2,500	15	6	4	8	9
2,501 - 5,000	17	11	7	13	12
5,001 - 10,000	23	19	18	20	28
>10,000	34	60	69	51	46

Q24D. Expenses — other

	AOG	SBC	CATH	LUTH	PRES
0 - 100	56	50	64	24	14
101 - 500	7	6	3	13	11
501 - 1,000	5	9	2	11	10
1,001 - 2,500	10	11	8	22	10
2,501 - 5,000	10	12	6	12	18
5,001 - 10,000	4	8	6	11	14
>10,000	7	5	12	8	23

Q24E. Total expenses

	AOG	SBC	CATH	LUTH	PRES
<50000	18	23	7	18	12
50,001 - 100,000	31	30	12	28	25
100,001 - 200,000	28	24	16	33	32
200,001 - 500,000	19	15	34	17	23
>500,000	4	9	31	4	9

Q25A. Congregation have mortgage?

	AOG	SBC	CATH	LUTH	PRES
Yes	62	47	32	37	23
No	38	54	68	63	77

Q25B. Annual mortgage payment

	AOG	SBC	CATH	LUTH	PRES
<2,000	18	51	23	14	44
2,001 - 5,000	13	4	2	5	9
5,001 - 10,000	13	7	10	16	11
10,001 - 25,000	21	23	11	32	7
>25,000	35	15	55	34	30

Q26. Who was involved in the preparation of the budget?

	AOG	SBC	CATH	LUTH	PRES
Pastor	77	82	94	82	82
Paid staff	20	39	52	18	24
Governing board	80	41	34	89	91
Finance committee	31	94	83	64	87
Cong members	10	46	8	26	28

Q27. Who has *final* say in approving the budget?

	AOG	SBC	CATH	LUTH	PRES
Pastor	16	0	69	0	0
Governing board	43	0	8	0	91
Finance committee	0	0	11	0	1
Cong members	25	98	0	100	6
Pastor & governing board	11	0	0	0	0
Pastor & finance comm	0	0	2	0	0
Pastor, board & finance board	2	0	6	0	0
Board & finance comm.	0	0	2	0	0
Other	3	2	1	0	2

Q28. What strategies were used to encourage lay giving to support the congregation's operating budget last year?

Q28A. Sermons on stewardship

	AOG	SBC	CATH	LUTH	PRES
Pastor only	70	64	41	67	69
Laypersons only	0	0	5	0	0
Pastor and laypersons	20	24	28	24	24
No sermons	10	12	26	9	7

Q28B. Appeals or testimonials during worship

	AOG	SBC	CATH	LUTH	PRES
Pastor only	15	10	30	4	5
Laypersons only	9	15	8	33	38
Pastor and laypersons	20	24	28	24	24
No appeals	14	23	30	29	13

Q28C. Distribute promotional material

	AOG	SBC	CATH	LUTH	PRES
At church only	22	33	19	4	9
Mailed to members only	3	2	8	7	9
At church and mailed	34	42	48	81	75
No promo material	41	23	26	8	7

Q28D. Phone every member

	AOG	SBC	CATH	LUTH	PRES
Pastor only	0	0	0	0	0
Laypersons only	1	1	3	4	8
Pastor and laypersons	7	2	0	1	1
Not phone	92	97	97	95	92

Q28E. Visit every member

	AOG	SBC	CATH	LUTH	PRES
Pastor only	4	0	0	0	0
Laypersons only	0	2	0	11	17
Pastor & laypersons	7	2	1	7	3
Not visit	89	96	99	82	80

Q28F. Phone some members

	AOG	SBC	CATH	LUTH	PRES
Pastor only	6	0	3	0	0
Laypersons only	0	2	10	16	30
Pastor and laypersons	7	5	5	3	5
Not do partial phone	87	93	82	81	65

Q28G. Visit some members

	AOG	SBC	CATH	LUTH	PRES
Pastors only	8	1	4	0	0
Laypersons only	1	3	3	15	22
Pastors and laypersons	6	8	9	7	8
Not visit	86	88	85	78	70

Q29. In your program to encourage giving, which had the greater emphasis?

	AOG	SBC	CATH	LUTH	PRES
Percent of income	66	45	19	40	23
Support programs	11	20	47	30	41
Half and half	15	25	19	24	29
No program	8	10	16	6	8

Q30. Did your congregation use any of the following?

	AOG	SBC	CATH	LUTH	PRES
Pledge cards	43	18	46	59	89
Numbered envelopes	19	65	94	93	87
Monthly/quarterly receipts	23	39	16	72	68
Annual receipts	77	61	50	67	68
Other	6	9	6	9	6

Q31. What procedures were used concerning mailing in contributions?

	AOG	SBC	CATH	LUTH	PRES
Postal envelope provided	1	2	8	10	17
Postal envelope not provided	86	90	81	90	83
Mailing discouraged	14	8	11	1	1

Q32. What is your congregation's emphasis with regard to the biblical standard of tithing?

	AOG	SBC	CATH	LUTH	PRES
Tithe due God	99	81	5	2	14
Tithe not obligatory	2	9	17	34	32
Proportion of income emphasized	0	7	58	58	42
Proportionate giving not emphasized	0	3	20	6	12

Q33. Which of the following is emphasized most strongly in your congregation?

	AOG	SBC	CATH	LUTH	PRES
Commit lives to Christ	50	54	5	10	21
Change society structures	0	1	3	2	8
Follow teachings of Jesus	50	45	62	63	67
Part in church tradition	0	0	30	25	3

Q34. What is your congregation's approach to interpreting and teaching the biblical meaning of Christian faith and the Church?

	AOG	SBC	CATH	LUTH	PRES
Our church true interpretation	79	65	83	24	7
One true interpretation	12	24	1	25	27
Many valid interpretations	9	11	16	51	66

Q35. Does your congregation teach that Christian life should be safeguarded through abstinence from:

	AOG	SBC	CATH	LUTH	PRES
Food	7	5	13	0	0
Alcohol/tobacco	94	85	4	4	5
Gambling	90	81	2	2	6
Movies/dancing	90	59	10	1	2
Other	25	31	37	8	18
None stressed	4	9	45	86	79

Q36. In general, how would you describe your congregation's teaching in relation to "typical" churches in your denomination?

	AOG	SBC	CATH	LUTH	PRES
Allows more differences	12	18	13	14	20
Similar to typical	79	75	80	83	58
Stricter	9	8	7	4	23

Q37. Last year what emphasis did you give to the biblical concept of stewardship of God's gifts?

	AOG	SBC	CATH	LUTH	PRES
Year-round	55	36	16	27	23
Occasional	45	58	44	64	66
Once	0	4	19	5	10
No emphasis	1	2	21	4	2

Q38. How was stewardship emphasized?

	AOG	SBC	CATH	LUTH	PRES
Sermons	96	94	70	91	92
Lay testimonials	66	59	28	51	65
Religious education	75	72	9	55	44
Church newsletter	51	56	65	89	87
Other	15	13	21	30	32

RESPONSES TO LAY QUESTIONNAIRES

This appendix gives percentage responses to all items on the lay question-naires. The number of cases were: Assemblies of God, 1,915; Southern Baptists, 1,883; Catholics, 2,194; Evangelical Lutheran Church of America, 2,470; and Presbyterians, 2,440. All the data were weighted to represent a random sample of laypersons in each denomination. Columns may not total to 100 because of rounding.

Q1. How long have you been attending worship services in your congregation?

	AOG	SBC	CATH	LUTH	PRES
Less than one year	6	3	2	2	1
1- 2 years	15	9	6	7	7
3-5 years	23	15	13	13	13
6-10 years	24	14	15	13	16
11-20 years	19	19	20	19	22
Over 20 years	13	41	45	47	42

Q2. Does your congregation have serious financial needs?

	AOG	SBC	CATH	LUTH	PRES
Yes, very serious	11	6	6	9	8
Yes, somewhat serious	29	31	33	38	32
No, only routine	42	50	38	40	45
No, financially well off	6	6	6	4	5
I don't know	12	6	18	10	9

Q3. Do you feel you have enough information about the handling and allocation of funds by the leaders of your congregation?

	AOG	SBC	CATH	LUTH	PRES
Yes	71	81	53	73	76
No	20	12	28	16	15
No opinion	9	8	19	10	9

Q4. Do you feel that typical members of your congregation have enough influence in decisions about the use of church money?

	AOG	SBC	CATH	LUTH	PRES
Yes	67	79	48	69	70
No	19	15	25	20	19
No opinion	14	7	27	11	11

Q5. How much do you trust the handling and allocation of funds by the leaders of your congregation?

	AOG	SBC	CATH	LUTH	PRES
High	81	81	66	69	73
Medium	17	18	31	28	26
Low	2	2	3	2	2

Q6. How much enthusiasm do you feel, in general, about the work and programs of your congregation?

	AOG	SBC	CATH	LUTH	PRES
Very high	33	26	17	16	22
Moderately high	49	52	51	55	56
Moderately low	12	16	18	19	16
Very low	3	3	6	5	4
Generally opposed	0	0	0	0	0
No opinion	3	3	8	6	3

Q7. In the last year did you, or another adult in your family, fill out a pledge card or commitment card regarding church giving for the year?

	AOG	SBC	CATH	LUTH	PRES
Yes	31	29	52	60	79
No	67	69	45	39	20
Don't know	2	2	3	2	1

Q8. Do you approve or disapprove of the practice of asking lay members of the congregation to fill out annual pledge cards or commitment cards regarding church giving for the year?

	AOG	SBC	CATH	LUTH	PRES
Approve	37	41	48	58	78
Disapprove	46	47	38	32	15
Don't know	17	12	14	10	7

Q9. Do you prefer that clergy (priests or ministers) or lay leaders handle financial matters in your congregation?

	AOG	SBC	CATH	LUTH	PRES
Clergy	3	1	10	1	1
Combination	82	65	78	68	68
Lay leaders	9	28	4	23	27
No preference	7	6	9	8	5

Q10. Has your congregation actively promoted a "stewardship approach" to the giving of time, talent, and money which teaches the spiritual meaning of how we use God's gifts?

	AOG	SBC	CATH	LUTH	PRES
Yes-give more	42	34	20	28	35
Yes-no effect	30	38	44	53	51
Yes-give less	0	0	1	1	1
No	15	17	10	8	6
Don't know	13	11	25	10	7

Q11. How do you make decisions about how much money to contribute to your congregation?

	AOG	SBC	CATH	LUTH	PRES
Tithe	73	44	4	7	9
Annual percent	3	7	6	8	9
Annual amount	2	9	14	22	41
Weekly amount	8	19	39	38	25
Can afford each week	15	22	37	26	15

Q12. Do you feel that lay members have sufficient influence on the decision-making in your denomination?

	AOG	SBC	CATH	LUTH	PRES
Yes	66	68	49	66	69
No	20	22	27	16	19
No opinion	14	10	24	18	12

Q13. Does your denomination as a whole (nationwide or worldwide) have serious financial needs?

	AOG	SBC	CATH	LUTH	PRES
Yes, very serious	4	9	13	7	10
Yes, somewhat	18	33	38	35	34
No, only routine	38	31	23	23	22
No, financially well off	3	2	7	2	2
Don't know	38	25	20	33	32

Q14. Do you feel you have enough information about the handling and allocation of funds by the leaders of your denomination?

	AOG	SBC	CATH	LUTH	PRES
Yes	54	51	34	46	46
No	27	33	46	33	36
No opinion	19	16	20	21	18

Q15. How much do you trust the handling and allocation of funds by the leaders of your denomination?

	AOG	SBC	CATH	LUTH	PRES
High	68	43	46	47	43
Medium	29	45	45	48	44
Low	2	13	9	6	13

Q16. For supporting mission projects of your denomination, either overseas or in this country, do you prefer that the denomination select and fund the mission projects or do you prefer that you select the mission projects to which to give?

	AOG	SBC	CATH	LUTH	PRES
Denomination	19	35	23	23	20
Self	25	16	31	20	25

Combination	51	43	36	46	49
No opinion	5	6	10	11	6

Q17. Do you read any magazines, newspapers, or newsletters published by your denomination or a denomination-related group (e.g., diocese, synod, association, or convention)?

	AOG	SBC	CATH	LUTH	PRES
Regularly	40	45	36	34	24
Occasionally	40	34	36	38	38
Rarely	11	12	17	18	20
No	9	9	11	10	17

Q18. How much enthusiasm do you feel, in general, about the work and programs of your denomination?

	AOG	SBC	CATH	LUTH	PRES
Very high	34	18	14	10	10
Moderately high	47	51	50	47	47
Moderately low	10	18	19	23	24
Very low	2	5	6	6	8
Generally opposed	0	1	0	1	1
No opinion	6	8	10	15	10

Q19. Would you prefer that congregations make more decisions about funding programs, such as missions, outreach, and social service, rather than having denominational leaders decide?

	AOG	SBC	CATH	LUTH	PRES
More local decision making	36	50	44	50	56
Like situation now	48	37	33	29	29
More denominational decision-making	3	4	4	3	3
No opinion	13	10	20	18	12

Q20. Only followers of Jesus Christ can be saved.

	AOG	SBC	CATH	LUTH	PRES
Strongly agree	83	77	21	34	33
Moderately agree	3	7	14	18	16
Neither	3	6	17	20	20

Moderately disagree	1	3	15	12	12
Strongly disagree	10	8	34	17	19

Q21. If I had to change the congregation I attend, I would feel a great sense of loss.

	AOG	SBC	CATH	LUTH	PRES
Strongly agree	51	51	39	36	39
Moderately agree	28	29	25	31	32
Neither	13	12	19	18	15
Moderately disagree	5	6	9	10	8
Strongly disagree	4	3	7	5	5

Q22. Opportunities to serve in lay leadership in my congregation are available if one is willing to make the commitment.

	AOG	SBC	CATH	LUTH	PRES
Strongly agree	73	79	63	68	70
Moderately agree	16	11	22	20	21
Neither	7	7	10	9	6
Moderately disagree	3	2	3	2	2
Strongly disagree	2	1	2	1	2

Q23. Important decisions about the life of my congregation are made with open discussion by church leaders and members.

	AOG	SBC	CATH	LUTH	PRES
Strongly agree	47	64	20	44	38
Moderately agree	25	23	27	33	35
Neither	13	7	31	12	13
Moderately disagree	8	4	12	7	8
Strongly disagree	7	3	10	4	6

Q24. The budget priorities of my congregation are appropriate.

	AOG	SBC	CATH	LUTH	PRES
Strongly agree	47	45	21	27	31
Moderately agree	27	35	32	42	41
Neither	19	11	37	18	17
Moderately disagree	5	6	7	8	8
Strongly disagree	3	3	3	4	3

Q25. My whole approach to life is based on my religion.

	AOG	SBC	CATH	LUTH	PRES
Strongly agree	75	59	40	31	31
Moderately agree	16	28	33	42	42
Neither	4	9	15	18	17
Moderately disagree	2	2	8	7	8
Strongly disagree	3	2	2	3	3

Q26. What religion offers me most is comfort in times of trouble and sorrow.

	AOG	SBC	CATH	LUTH	PRES
Strongly agree	33	34	38	30	22
Moderately agree	25	28	28	31	32
Neither	17	15	16	18	19
Moderately disagree	11	12	11	13	17
Strongly disagree	14	12	8	7	11

Q27. The leaders of my congregation are sufficiently accountable to members regarding how church contributions are used.

	AOG	SBC	CATH	LUTH	PRES
Strongly agree	58	63	30	45	46
Moderately agree	22	24	31	36	36
Neither	12	8	28	14	12
Moderately disagree	5	3	7	4	5
Strongly disagree	3	2	5	2	2

Q28. The leaders of my denomination are sufficiently accountable to members regarding how church contributions are used.

	AOG	SBC	CATH	LUTH	PRES
Strongly agree	39	27	18	21	18
Moderately agree	23	29	26	29	26
Neither	31	28	34	39	36
Moderately disagree	5	10	12	8	11
Strongly disagree	3	7	9	4	10

Q29. Overall, the pastor of my congregation is doing a good job.

	AOG	SBC	CATH	LUTH	PRES
Strongly agree	77	70	62	62	66
Moderately agree	16	19	25	24	22
Neither	3	5	7	7	7
Moderately disagree	3	3	4	4	3
Strongly disagree	2	3	2	3	3

Q30. Overall, the leadership of my denomination is doing a good job.

	AOG	SBC	CATH	LUTH	PRES
Strongly agree	56	29	34	28	22
Moderately agree	26	31	37	38	32
Neither	5	19	18	28	32
Moderately disagree	2	11	7	4	9
Strongly disagree	2	10	5	2	6

Q31. Overall, I approve of the decision-making process in my congregation.

	AOG	SBC	CATH	LUTH	PRES
Strongly agree	60	59	32	40	45
Moderately agree	24	29	40	41	40
Neither	8	6	19	11	8
Moderately disagree	6	5	6	6	5
Strongly disagree	2	2	3	2	2

Q32. Overall, I approve of the decision-making process in my denomination.

	AOG	SBC	CATH	LUTH	PRES
Strongly agree	43	23	21	19	17
Moderately agree	27	29	33	35	32
Neither	8	6	19	11	8
Moderately disagree	6	5	6	6	5
Strongly disagree	2	2	3	2	2

Q33. What do you believe the *primary* duty of Christians is?

	AOG	SBC	CATH	LUTH	PRES
Help others commit to Christ	60	56	6	14	16
Change unjust social structure	0	1	6	4	6
Follow teachings of Jesus	38	41	60	63	66
Participate in traditions and sacraments	0	1	22	11	5
Don't know	2	2	6	7	7

Q34. How often do you attend worship services at your church?

	AOG	SBC	CATH	LUTH	PRES
Never	0	1	1	1	1
Few times/year	1	3	6	8	8
Once/month	1	1	4	9	7
2 to 3 times/month	5	8	11	27	25
once/week	27	36	59	51	53
>once/week	66	51	20	4	7

Q35. How many hours, if any, during the last month have you attended programs or events at your church other than worship services?

	AOG	SBC	CATH	LUTH	PRES
0	14	9	51	37	32
1-2	11	8	23	22	18
3-5	28	27	14	24	24
6-10	24	32	8	12	17
11-20	13	16	3	4	6
>20	10	8	1	2	2

Q36. How many hours, if any, during the last month have you given volunteer time at your church to teach, lead, serve on a committee, or help with some program, event, or task?

	AOG	SBC	CATH	LUTH	PRES
0	31	25	63	45	41
1-2	16	17	13	19	20
3-5	21	24	12	19	19
6-10	18	19	6	12	13
11-20	8	10	4	3	5
>20	7	6	2	2	3

During the last year, approximately how much money did your household contribute to each of the following? Write your best estimate in the boxes provided and fill in the corresponding circles underneath. Use only whole dollar amounts; do not use "cents."

Q37. To your church, in regular giving (not including school tuition or contributions to a capital campaign). Include the value of material goods as well as monetary gifts.

	AOG	SBC	CATH	LUTH	PRES
0	1	2	2	2	2
1-100	3	4	9	9	6
101-250	4	4	12	10	8
251-500	8	9	25	18	17
501-1,000	12	14	32	22	22
1,001-2,500	31	31	15	28	29
2,501-5,000	28	25	3	9	13
5,001-10,000	11	10	1	2	3
>10,000	2	1	0	0	1

Q38. To your church, in giving to a special capital campaign for a new building or a new program.

	AOG	SBC	CATH	LUTH	PRES
0	50	50	47	54	50
1-100	19	17	26	20	15
101-250	9	9	13	8	10
251-500	12	12	7	8	11
501-1,000	6	6	4	6	7
1,001-2,500	3	4	2	3	5
2,501-5,000	1	1	0	1	1
5,001-10,000	0	1	0	1	1
>10,000	0	0	0	0	1

Q39. During the last year, approximately how much money did your household contribute to groups or causes in your denomination other than those described in questions 37 and 38?

	AOG	SBC	CATH	LUTH	PRES
0	18	21	18	28	26
1-50	24	30	34	35	31
51-100	19	19	19	17	17

101-500	26	23	21	15	20
501-1,000	7	5	5	2	3
1,001-2,000	3	2	2	1	1
>2,000	2	2	2	1	1

Q40. During the last year, approximately how much money did your household contribute to all religious groups or causes outside your denomination?

	AOG	SBC	CATH	LUTH	PRES
0	27	36	33	35	30
1-50	27	29	34	33	26
51-100	13	11	14	12	13
101-500	19	15	15	14	17
501-1,000	6	5	3	4	6
1,001-2,000	4	3	2	2	4
>2,000	4	2	1	1	4

Q41. During the last year, approximately how much money did your household contribute to non-religious charities, community organizations or social causes?

	AOG	SBC	CATH	LUTH	PRES
0	20	10	9	5	5
1-50	40	32	29	29	22
51-100	17	21	22	23	18
101-500	19	26	29	30	35
501-1,000	3	8	7	8	11
1,001-2,000	1	2	2	3	5
>2, 000	1	1	2	2	5

Are there situations under which you might consider donating more money to your congregation? I would give more money to my congregation if:

Q42. It were more spiritually nourishing

	AOG	SBC	CATH	LUTH	PRES
Yes	12	13	16	13	14
No	70	63	54	58	62
Don't know	18	24	30	29	24

Q43. The preaching were more meaningful

	AOG	SBC	CATH	LUTH	PRES
Yes	8	8	16	11	11
No	78	73	60	66	69
Don't know	14	19	24	24	20

Q44. It paid more attention to social issues

	AOG	SBC	CATH	LUTH	PRES
Yes	5	8	16	10	11
No	83	76	57	68	71
Don't know	12	17	27	22	18

Q45. It paid less attention to social issues

	AOG	SBC	CATH	LUTH	PRES
Yes	2	3	5	4	6
No	87	81	70	75	75
Don't know	10	15	21	20	16

Q46. The worship services were more traditional

	AOG	SBC	CATH	LUTH	PRES
Yes	4	5	12	7	7
No	87	80	67	73	77
Don't know	10	15	21	20	16

Q47. The worship services were more modern

	AOG	SBC	CATH	LUTH	PRES
Yes	2	2	8	5	4
No	88	84	72	75	80
Don't know	9	14	20	20	17

Q48. What is your sex?

	AOG	SBC	CATH	LUTH	PRES
Female	56	59	62	63	62
Male	44	41	38	37	38

Q49. What is your age?

	AOG	SBC	CATH	LUTH	PRES
<18					
18-25	0	0	0	0	0
26-30	3	2	1	1	1
31-35	7	4	4	4	3
36-40	14	11	12	10	9
41-45	15	11	10	10	12
46-50	11	9	10	10	8
51-55	8	8	8	10	8
56-60	8	9	8	8	7
61-65	7	10	10	10	10
66-75	10	18	18	17	20
>75	4	9	10	11	14

Q50. How would you describe yourself?

	AOG	SBC	CATH	LUTH	PRES
Asian/Pacific Islander	1	0	5	0	0
African-American	2	1	1	0	2
Hispanic	5	0	5	0	0
White	91	96	88	99	97
Naive-American	1	1	0	0	0
Biracial	1	1	1	0	0

Q51. Which of the following best applies to you currently?

	AOG	SBC	CATH	LUTH	PRES
Single	6	4	8	5	6
Committed relationship	1	1	1	1	1
Married	79	78	71	78	74
Separated	2	0	1	1	0
Divorced	6	5	6	5	5
Widowed	7	13	13	11	14

Q52. If you are currently married or living in a committed relationship, does your partner attend the same congregation you do?

	AOG	SBC	CATH	LUTH	PRES
Yes	72	73	64	72	67
No	9	8	12	9	11
Does not apply	18	19	25	19	23

Q53. What is your highest level of education?

	AOG	SBC	CATH	LUTH	PRES
High school or less	34	29	28	28	16
Some college	41	39	32	35	31
College grad	17	20	20	22	30
Graduate degree	8	12	20	15	23

Q54. About how much income did your family or household receive last year from all sources before taxes?

	AOG	SBC	CATH	LUTH	PRES
<10,000	8	6	8	6	4
10,000-14,999	9	8	9	9	6
15,000-19,999	9	7	7	8	7
20,000-29,999	18	17	17	16	13
30,000-39,999	18	16	14	17	16
40,000-49,999	13	14	13	14	12
50,000-59,999	10	14	10	10	13
60,000-69,999	6	7	7	7	8
70,000-79,999	4	6	4	5	6
80,000-99,999	3	4	5	5	7
100,000-149,999	1	2	4	3	6
>or=150,000	1	1	3	2	4

Q55. How many dependent children (under 18 years of age) do you have living with you?

	AOG	SBC	CATH	LUTH	PRES
0	52	65	60	65	68
1	15	11	13	10	11
2	19	17	16	16	16
3	9	6	7	7	5
>or=4	4	2	5	2	1

Q56. How many dependent children (under 18 years of age) in your household attend religiously affiliated grammar school or high school (Catholic, Lutheran, etc.) five days a week?

	AOG	SBC	CATH	LUTH	PRES
0	89	96	87	97	97
1	7	2	7	2	2
2	4	1	3	1	1
3	1	1	1	1	1
>or=4	1	0	1	0	0

INDEX

ABOUT THE AUTHOR

Charles E. Zech, a Notre Dame graduate, is a professor of economics at Villanova University. Out of his research have come two previous books, *Plain Talk About Churches and Money* (with Dean Hoge and Patrick McNamara), and *Money Matters: Personal Giving in American Churches* (with Dean Hoge, Patrick McNamara, and Michael Donahue). He is the author of dozens of articles, and has spoken to many parish groups, on the topic of giving.

Our Sunday Visitor ...
Your Source for Discovering
the Riches of the Catholic Faith

Our Sunday Visitor has an extensive line of materials for young children, teens, and adults. Our books, Bibles, pamphlets, CD-ROMs, audios, and videos are available in bookstores worldwide.

To receive a FREE full-line catalog or for more information, call **Our Sunday Visitor** at **1-800-348-2440, ext. 3**. Or write **Our Sunday Visitor** / 200 Noll Plaza / Huntington, IN 46750.

Please send me ___ A catalog
Please send me materials on:
___ Apologetics and catechetics
___ Prayer books
___ The family
___ Reference works
___ Heritage and the saints
___ The parish

Name _____
Address _____ Apt._____
City _____ State _____ Zip_____
Telephone (   ) _____
                                                    A63BBBBP

Please send a friend ___ A catalog
Please send a friend materials on:
___ Apologetics and catechetics
___ Prayer books
___ The family
___ Reference works
___ Heritage and the saints
___ The parish

Name _____
Address _____ Apt._____
City _____ State _____ Zip_____
Telephone (   ) _____
                                                    A63BBBBP

OurSundayVisitor

200 Noll Plaza, Huntington, IN 46750
Toll free: **1-800-348-2440**
Website: www.osv.com